changing
patterns

changing patterns

DISCOVERING THE FABRIC
OF YOUR CREATIVITY

Daena Giardella *and* **Wren Ross**

HAY HOUSE, INC.
Carlsbad, California
London • Sydney • Johannesburg
Vancouver • Hong Kong

Published and distributed in the United States by: Hay House, Inc., P.O. Box 5100, Carlsbad, CA 92018-5100 • *Phone:* (760) 431-7695 or (800) 654-5126 • *Fax:* (760) 431-6948 or (800) 650-5115 • www.hayhouse.com • **Published and distributed in Australia by:** Hay House Australia Pty. Ltd., 18/36 Ralph St., Alexandria NSW 2015 • *Phone:* 612-9669-4299 • *Fax:* 612-9669-4144 • www.hayhouse.com.au • **Published and distributed in the United Kingdom by:** Hay House UK, Ltd. • Unit 62, Canalot Studios • 222 Kensal Rd., London W10 5BN • *Phone:* 44-20-8962-1230 • *Fax:* 44-20-8962-1239 • www.hay house.co.uk • **Published and distributed in the Republic of South Africa by:** Hay House SA (Pty), Ltd., P.O. Box 990, Witkoppen 2068 • *Phone/Fax:* 27-11-706-6612 • orders@psdprom.co.za • **Distributed in Canada by:** Raincoast • 9050 Shaughnessy St., Vancouver, B.C. V6P 6E5 • *Phone:* (604) 323-7100 • *Fax:* (604) 323-2600

Design: Chris Ventzos • *Interior Design:* Tricia Breidenthal • *Knot Illustrations:* Joni Coniglio • *Photo "Web Sight" page 101:* Russ Campbell • *Photo "Knitting Meditation" page 184:* George Schlossnagle

All of the other photographs used in this book were taken by Daena Giardella and can be purchased as photo cards or enlargements at: **www.daenagiardella.com.**

Library of Congress Cataloging-in-Publication Data

Giardella, Daena.
  Changing patterns : discovering the fabric of your creativity / Daena Giardella and Wren Ross.
    p. cm.
  ISBN-13: 978-1-4019-0756-3 (tradepaper)
  ISBN-10: 1-4019-0756-3 (tradepaper)
  1. Creative ability. I. Ross, Wren. II. Title.
  BF408.G43 2006
  153.3'5--dc22
                                        2005024302

ISBN 13: 978-1-4019-0756-3
ISBN 10: 1-4019-0756-3

09 08 07 06   4 3 2 1
1st printing, January 2006

Printed in the United Kingdom by Lightning Source.

We dedicate this book to Molly . . .

*and to the curious 5-year-old and the wise
99-year-old within all of us, who encourage us
to take risks, express freely, and create boldly.*

contents

preface

A Compass for the Journey

We wrote this book because we share a common passion: creativity. A deep love and respect for the creative process has strongly motivated each of our life paths. Daena is an actor, creativity coach, motivational speaker, teacher, writer, and photographer; her specialty is the art of improvisation. Wren is a singer, voice-over actor, teacher, writer, designer, and longtime knitter—she loves the nuances of color.

We've worked together in the creation of many original theater performances and cabarets. In our acting workshops, private-coaching sessions, and organizational-training seminars, we help people speak and act with confidence, freedom, and authenticity. Over the years, we've realized that creativity is a profound practice for personal growth, because the creative process reveals each person's habitual patterns and offers a potent opportunity for conscious change.

There have been separate books gestating within each of us for many years. Since our work is so intertwined, we've always joked that our books would probably want to sit next to each other on the bookshelf. Eventually, a lightbulb flashed: Why not give our readers both books between one set of covers? Our concept quickly came into sharp focus.

Changing Patterns: Discovering the Fabric of Your Creativity is really two books in one. Each half could stand alone, but together they reflect the interconnectedness and synergy of our work. As Aristotle said, "The whole is more than the sum of its parts."

At the beginning of our collaboration on this book, we had many brainstorming sessions around the kitchen table. One morning we sat in a wash of December light savoring our last bites of oatmeal as we discussed our vision for the book. Our black cat, Molly, sat on the chair beside us. . . .

Daena: Have you noticed that we often end up talking at the kitchen table?

Wren: Yes! Maybe it's a cultural thing. You're Italian. . . .

Daena: And you're Jewish . . . and this is where our people have congregated for eons.

Wren: Maybe it has something to do with the hearth—we come to the kitchen to nurture our ideas and ourselves.

Daena: So now we're cooking up a book.

Wren: Okay, you'll write the first half of the book about the creative process as a tool for self-discovery and change.

Daena: And you'll write the second half about knitting as a metaphor for life.

Wren: Creativity brings meaning to each person's life.

Daena: Absolutely. A deficit of meaning and purpose is often underneath many emotional problems and life struggles. Psychotherapists and life coaches often encourage people to bring more creativity to their lives. Creativity is good medicine. I'd like my part of *Changing Patterns* to be a guidebook for everyone who wants to discover or recover their creative process. I want to help people from all walks of life ignite and sustain the fires of their creativity. Life can be more vibrant, purposeful, and satisfying when these fires are lit.

Wren: I agree. Every art form can be a path of self-awareness.

Daena: Whether someone is weaving a tapestry or writing a novel . . .

Wren: Or choreographing a new dance piece . . .

Daena: Creativity is an intimate companion that offers a microcosm of life's essential lessons.

Wren: Although you and I have backgrounds in the performing arts, I think it would be useful to illustrate the power of the creative process by looking at the art of knitting in this book. Knitting is accessible, tangible, and popular. In the second part of *Changing Patterns,* I'd like to discuss the ways that knitting can bring the reader more self-reflection, fulfillment, and peace. The process of knitting is calming and centering; it's a meditation and a great metaphor for life because it teaches a person how to make connections effectively. We become more skilled in maneuvering our mistakes, tangles, beginnings, endings, and well . . . the very fiber of life.

〰️

And so we set off on our writing journey. Early in the process, the theme of compassion kept arising as we spoke about what mattered most to us. This quality is vital as you contemplate your relationship to creativity. When we noticed that the word *compassion* has the words *compass* and *passion* within it, we realized immediately that this was a wonderful expression of our intention: We want our book to be a compassionate compass for people as they embark on their creative adventures with passion and delight. We invite you to bring along compassion as *your* compass.

— **Daena Giardella** and **Wren Ross**

introduction

Creating Change

Your creative process is a powerful path of self-development that gives you the opportunity to learn about yourself and express your deepest potential. Each time you create something, you're also re-creating yourself.

Have you ever noticed that you feel different after you've finished writing a poem, painting a landscape, performing onstage, playing the piano, or knitting a scarf? The sense of completion is satisfying, but there's something more: You literally activate the atoms and cells of your brain and body during the creation process as your neurotransmitters carry many messages of insight and discovery. You wake up, plug in, get connected, and manifest your vision. You give birth to something that contains a piece of your essence. The creating self is created anew with each act of creation.

As you create, you change. You bump up against emotional patterns and recurring roadblocks, acquire new skills and dexterity in your craft, and learn how to solve problems and improvise alternatives. You expand your consciousness by leaving behind the deadening drone of modern media imagery and switching on the inner channels of your imagination. Creativity changes you from a passive consumer to an inspired activist.

The art of knitting has been around for many centuries. In recent years, it's enjoyed a tremendous explosion of interest, and it seems as if people everywhere are picking up needles and yarn to create garments that they'd rather make than buy. Virtually every family has someone—a grandmother, mother, aunt, brother, or niece—who knits. Mention the word *knitting* to someone and within seconds a warm smile and fond story will spring forth: "My grandmother used to knit sweaters for everyone" or "My mom is a compulsive knitter—she taught me when I was nine."

In addition to being a wonderfully soothing activity, the practice of knitting is rich in life metaphors. How you learn, what you encounter while working on projects, and how you develop mastery reveal useful lessons about living: *As you knit, you change.* A single strand of yarn becomes a piece of fabric, and simultaneously, you become more relaxed and aware. Knitting clears the mind and opens the heart. Knitters are revolutionaries—they knit in quiet, steady rebellion against life's racing pace.

We want this book to be a practical and stimulating springboard for your personal exploration. We decided to join these two complementary investigations: the creative process and knitting as vehicles for self-awareness in everyday life. We quickly realized that this would be a book about changing patterns and discovering the fabric of your creativity.

In Part I, Daena explores the creative process as a vital tool for self-discovery and fulfillment. What is the creative process? How can you develop your creativity and make it a regular practice? Where do you find inspiration, and what happens if you get lost or confused? What are the universal psychological stages in every act of creation? What are your personal cycles? How can you change habitual patterns that get in your way, deal with nagging inner-critic voices, and overcome blocks? What can you do about resistance? What can nature teach you about creativity? What's your relationship to structure and improvisation, and how can you have more fun with it all?

In Part II, Wren invites you to experience the power of the creative process using knitting as a metaphor for life. Why knit? What is knitting? What are the hidden transformational meanings of knots? How is this practice a meditation—do you have to be patient? What's your relationship to beginnings and endings? What's in a knitter's mind, and what are knitting intentions? How do you deal with your mistakes? How do you get into and out of tangles? How do you work with your tension? What about knitting patterns and life patterns? How did this fiber tradition begin, and why is it so popular now? What can you learn about yourself by practicing knitting as a contemplative and creative craft?

Finally, we'll leave you with a story about the awesome power of nature (the ultimate creativity guru). We invite you to keep a journal with your thoughts, feelings, and ideas as you read. You can begin by using the blank pages at the back of this book. You might also want to use the photos in each chapter to spark your imagination and help you think about your creative process. See the instructions in the section entitled *Your Creativity Journal* to find suggestions for how to engage in a *photo dialogue* with each image.

Bon voyage—enjoy the journey!

PART I

Exploring Your Creative Process

by Daena Giardella

chapter 1

What Is the Creative Process?

> *"Creativity is piercing the*
> *mundane to find the marvelous."*
> — Bill Moyers

The creative process is a passionate, sweaty dance around a midnight bonfire. It's a deep-sea diving adventure and a trip to the moon. It's hard work and rewarding play. It's an intentional accident, a curious experiment, and an awesome discovery. It's a labor of love and a breeding ground for resistance. It's the careful act of putting commas and dashes where they belong, and it's a full can of paint flung at a canvas. It's the struggle to find the next word, and the riot police who show up to quell an unruly sentence that refuses to end. It's a mirror, a meditation, a mirage, and a mountain. It's a pack of galloping wild horses and the drip of a leaky pipe. It's a tenacious tangle with *No,* a defiant shuffle toward *Maybe,* and every cell in your body cheering *Yes!* as you jump off the edge.

The creative process is your best friend and worst enemy. It's always available to you, but sometimes it hides for days.

It's your identical twin echoing your innermost thoughts, and a total stranger staring impatiently at you from a blank page. It's an irrepressible urge to investigate and a quiet impulse to imagine. The creative process is your lover, your jailer, your secret confidant, and your forgiving therapist. It's a cosmic shape-shifter and a steady stream, a jumbled muddle and a disciplined routine. It's a gangsta thug who raps inside your brain if you ignore him too long, an act of communion, and a soothing balm. It's an icy breakup, a steamy hot affair, an effortless climax, and a hallelujah chorus. It's a stint in solitary confinement and a crowd of cheering ideas. It's a torture chamber and a merciless judge. It's an exquisite epiphany and a cement crypt that won't budge. It's a thousand ice-cream cones and a sky full of fireworks. But more than anything, your creative process is a profound life teacher, a sacred vessel to express your soul purpose, and a wellspring of healing.

Creativity is an essential drive in human nature. The origin of this impulse may have been necessity—for example, learning to make fire helped the cave dwellers survive—but there's more to the story. Why did those early people carve drawings on their walls? The human imagination instinctively seeks expression, and creativity nourishes the soul. In modern life, the serious pursuit of creativity is often seen as something exclusively reserved for professional artists, while for everyone else it's "just a little hobby."

The hustle and bustle of the daily grind can leave little room for our imagination and inventive spirit to take flight. When we do have free time, the popular re*creation* of choice is passive entertainment, sitting in front of a TV watching others create or becoming glued to the virtual reality of our computer screens.

But what if you view the practice of creativity as a vital aspect of living that helps you understand and express who you truly are? When you make space for a regular creative practice, you exercise your brain, release stress, and increase your ability to meet life's challenges with flexibility, resourcefulness, and confidence. Let's look at the four cornerstones of creativity: process, purpose, passion, and curiosity.

Process

Creativity and process are inseparable. A process is a series of actions that contributes to a desired result. The word comes from the French word *procés,* which means "journey." For me, a journey is very different from a trip, which is something we do for business or other obligations. I like my trips to be as short as possible. A journey, however, is an adventure or a quest for meaning. While a trip focuses on quick results, a journey tells a story. When I go on a journey, I usually want to stretch it out as long as possible so that I can savor every moment. I love to be stimulated by new places and experiences that are off the beaten path, far from the usual tourist destinations. I always meet colorful characters who inspire me to learn something unexpected about the world or myself.

Do you remember taking a journey that you wished would never end? Creativity is such a path. While the outcome is crucial, the juicy experience lies in *how you get there.* In our results-driven world, the immense value of the process can sometimes be overshadowed. The creative process includes your methods, techniques, and artistic choices; it's a narrative of your journey from conception to outcome.

Every act of creation—whether it's a film, book, painting, building design, play, new business, or clay pot—has a rich backstory. The backstory always reveals a fascinating tapestry full of the dreams, dramas, feelings, obstacles, breakdowns, breakthroughs, and unshakable vision that coalesced to give birth to a particular creation. I love watching documentaries about the making of a film because they're often as interesting as the movie itself. Learning the story behind the story can be captivating because it sheds light on how the artists arrived at their decisions or shaped their images.

People often ask me about the backstory of my creative process after I perform one of my original theater pieces, so sometimes I include a third act where audience members ask questions about how I created the characters or story lines. I gain personal insights by looking back on my process and noticing what was happening in my life while I was developing each new production. I've learned that my story offstage usually makes its way into my themes and choices onstage. Even though I was present for the entire process of creation, I'm always surprised by how I got from here to there. The mystery of the journey never ceases to amaze me.

While I was living in Tel Aviv during the first Gulf War, I received a daily crash course in the art of living with gas masks and air-raid sirens as Scud missiles fell around us. I felt compelled to channel all the tumult, uncertainty, and absurdity into theater, and the gas mask I relied upon for safety became a central prop in my performance. My creative process was merged with my day-to-day experiences living in the pressure cooker of potential danger while continuing ordinary chores and activities. On countless occasions, I'd be startled from sleep by the sound of the siren commanding me to grab my mask groggily and go to the "safe room" we'd prepared to protect us from the unthinkable possibility of chemical weapons. A few hours later I might be teaching a workshop, buying vegetables at the market, laughing at an Israeli comedian on TV, or stirring a pot of rice in the quiet calm of the early evening. I learned the practical necessity of being in the

JOURNEY

moment, so I called my new show *Moment to Moment,* which was exactly how life needed to be lived in those weeks.

During my frequent visits to bomb shelters, I befriended many unforgettable children, former army officers, teenagers, artists, mothers, fathers, doctors, Holocaust survivors, engineers, and musicians. I cherished the resilient humanity of each person I met, and every encounter provided inspiration for a character or story in my performance. The sounds, sights, events, spices, cultures, and poetic beauty of this tiny patch of land by the sea profoundly influenced my process of creation. The complicated intersection of ancient legacies and modern contradictions rubbed against each other in my imagination. My life journey had given birth to an unexpected creative journey.

Think about a specific creative project you've undertaken and then write about the journey of your process. What methods, techniques, and choices contributed to it? Do you remember the backstory? What was happening in your life as you created, and what were you feeling? Identify the significant people or "characters" who participated in the plot of your creative endeavor. Who or what has inspired you? How was this backstory reflected in your creation? As you explore the process of your creativity, my hope is that you'll deepen your understanding and appreciation of your unique journey.

Purpose

The creative process is a laboratory for the expression of our greatest potential and the fulfillment of our life purpose.

Each of us feels a longing to connect with the rich possibilities of our personal aspirations. We sense that beyond the hurried activities of our schedules, there's a deeper intention that gives meaning to our lives. We want to express our talents, qualities, and inner spirit, and our creativity offers a path for this calling.

Every time we create something, we're touching the place where our intuitive feelings of purpose and meaning live. We're expressing our innermost self as we learn to master the materials of our craft. Creativity stimulates us to discover who we are, why we're here, and what matters to us. It transports us from the mundane to the meaningful as we dare to imagine what's possible.

In addition to its benefits for self-development, creativity is rapidly becoming the essential skill base for the 21st century. In his book *A Whole New Mind,* business author Daniel Pink observes, "The future belongs to a very different kind of person with a very different kind of mind—creators and empathizers, pattern recognizers and meaning makers. These people—artists, inventors, designers, storytellers, caregivers, consolers, big picture thinkers—will now reap society's richest rewards and share its greatest joys."

We stand at the threshold of an unprecedented time in human history. Each day brings fresh examples of our parallel capacities for creation and destruction that boggle the mind. Our achievements have brought us the promise of remarkable breakthroughs and advances in art, science, technology, and medicine. At the same time, the specter of global warming looms, as we seem incapable or unwilling to produce healthy, clean, and safe fuel alternatives. The by-products of our "progress" have polluted precious natural resources, including the water and air. Whether we're looking at the issues of obesity, poverty, disease, or violence, one thing is certain: We need dedicated and inspired creative minds to solve our problems. We need to become freethinkers who can contribute wisely and tangibly to the next chapters of our human story. We need to become compassionate innovators. Creativity is our ticket to participate in the exciting experiments of civilization and collective change.

Passion

As a young girl I wanted to be either an astronomer or an actor—the stars in the sky as well the ones in the movies and theater mesmerized me. Each day I'd spring out of bed with new ideas for quirky characters that I practiced in front of the bathroom mirror. My passion for inventing stories also found expression in my fascination with looking at the moon, stars, and planets through my trusty telescope. I would sit for hours, imagining how those celestial bodies got there and what it might be like to visit them. I became an actor, but I continue to learn about physics and astronomy every chance I get.

Over the years, I've spent a lot of time with both artists and scientists, and I've always been struck by the fact that even though their fields are quite different, they share a similar passion. They each possess a feisty dedication to uncover the truth, as well as highly developed intuitive feelings and instincts.

Scientists, artists, entrepreneurs, and other innovators are all motivated by emotion. Whether it's the thrill of discovering a medical cure, the joy of creating a new business solution, or the excitement of revealing the human condition through a dramatic character, the creative mind is fueled by emotion. Emotion is energy in motion. We're moved to do something when our passion is stirred. Love, joy, enthusiasm, and a sense of awe catalyze our imagination. Sometimes the energizing feelings might be frustration, pain, or even grief. Countless architects and designers were stirred by a profound need to conceptualize new buildings, memorials, and parks to fill the void after the tragedy of September 11, 2001.

Creativity is an expression of passion, the primal force of invention. When our passion is flowing freely, we're vibrating at a higher octave of intelligence, which gives us access to a greater sense of interconnectedness and insight. Award-winning neurologist and author Antonio Damasio has extensively researched the effects of neurobiology on language, memory, consciousness, and creativity. His books *Descartes' Error, The Feeling of What Happens,* and *Looking for Spinoza* are popular among lay readers, as well as scientists.

Dr. Damasio has shown that *emotion plays a crucial role in decision-making.* He says, "What you're really doing in the process of creating is choosing one thing over another, not necessarily because it is factually more positive but because it attracts you more. Emotion is literally the alarm that permits the detection." This means that your passion guides you as you create.

The creative process is essentially a series of ideas, problems, and choices that are driven by your passion. What are you passionate about? Do you give yourself permission to be passionate? Do you have creative outlets that enable you to give shape and form to your passion? Creativity benefits from a balance of keen intellectual abilities and well-developed emotional instincts. Do you squelch feelings that arise as you're creating? Imagine looking at your emotions as the essential igniters of your creative process. Passion sparks innovation, and your mission is to dedicate the energy behind your emotions to the service of your creativity. Where do you begin? As scholar and writer Joseph Campbell said, "Follow your bliss."

Curiosity

Creativity enables us to look at the world with awakened eyes. When we apply creative insight to the world around us, we see the poetry buried in everyday occurrences. This greater awareness energizes our life and stimulates our curiosity. And at the heart of everything creative is the delicious nectar of curiosity. No matter how much we drink from its cup, we always want more. Curiosity triggers our creative pursuits. Albert Einstein once said, "I have no special talents. I am only passionately curious." We all know how far his passionate curiosity transported him!

Curiosity is an eagerness to know, learn, acquire skills, gather information, and experiment. Our creative process is a sanctuary for this enthusiasm. The creative mind ponders the same five questions that a child asks: Why? How? Who? When? Where? We've all interacted with children who ask these questions over and over again—and sometimes they stump the adults who frantically search for an elusive answer. Our fascination with these meaningful queries often wanes as we grow into adulthood and get caught up in the practicalities of life. Time-management courses are far more popular than physics seminars on the origin of time.

As we become more focused on day-to-day logistics, our grasp on the deeper meaning of those five big questions might loosen. Sadly, this often results in the common modern malady of feeling bored or oversaturated with to-do lists, information, and externally generated images. We become passive and disinterested . . . but there's hope: Our creative process is a refuge where we can cultivate our vital need to wonder and express. It's a special personal space for experimenting with new ideas or practicing a skill—a pathway for finding a simple way to do something original or better. Most

WISH

important, our creative process is a repository for our *internally* generated images and ideas.

Your creative process is a link in a long line of creation that began with the emergence of the universe itself and continues through the countless achievements of human invention and art. The inspiration of each creator who preceded you is evoked by your present intention. I think of creative intention as both a sacred invocation and a hopeful invitation.

Imagine a place where you can draw upon the inspiration of every creative soul who has ever walked on Earth. When you consciously engage your creative process, you enter such a place. It's like venturing into a special church, temple, mosque, or kiva where creativity has been honored and celebrated for centuries. Envision sitting down in this extraordinary space and calling upon the artistic genius of Leonardo da Vinci or the passionate honesty of Frida Kahlo. Before beginning your creative activities, try closing your eyes as you quietly speak your invocation aloud. For example, you might say, "I invoke the brilliance, courage, humor, or insight of _____." Give yourself permission to get specific about inviting the qualities you need for that stage of your process.

Each time you create, you're invoking the inspiration, skills, and support that will help you manifest your ideas. You're also inviting your curiosity to feast at a sumptuous banquet in the home of your imagination.

The Wonderment Experiment

I love the state of wonderment that arises when I contemplate the mysteries of the night sky or experience an "Aha" moment during a creative investigation. I delight in any chance to marvel at something beautiful, surprising, or prolific. The exquisite beauty of the red-rock mountains and luminous blue skies of the American Southwest send chills down my spine. I can remember gasping aloud in a rush of amazement the first time I saw the Grand Canyon. I recognize this affinity for wonder as an expression of my curiosity.

I believe that curiosity is the ultimate medicine for a cynical, apathetic world. I'm reminded of the great humorist Dorothy Parker who quipped, "The cure for boredom is curiosity. There is no cure for curiosity." When we allow ourselves to wonder why or how, we arouse our senses and wake up to what might be possible.

Try an exercise that I call the *wonderment experiment:* Go somewhere with a conscious intention to exercise your curiosity. Take a walk in nature, go to a museum, or visit a zoo with fresh eyes, ears, and mind. Engage your appetite for wonderment. What would you like to learn? Do you understand why, how, when, where, and who? Find a naturalist, museum employee, or zookeeper who might be able to answer your questions, and allow your first inquiries to spawn new ones. Next, notice the images, sounds, or objects that you're drawn to the most. Is there a theme? Do you recognize yourself in these expressions of nature? As Goethe said in *Faust,* "Everything is a metaphor." Observe the world around you, and look for metaphors that reflect your life story.

I coached a woman named Kate who'd been feeling terribly stuck in her work and life—she yearned for a change and continually talked about her desire for transformation. I suggested that she try the wonderment experiment, and she chose to go to a wooded conservation area near her home. Here's what Kate described:

It was a Friday after work, when I was totally drained and depressed about my job and my horrible boss. I wasn't feeling particularly curious about anything except maybe sleep. But I remembered that I'd agreed to try your experiment, so I mustered up as much curiosity as I could and walked in the woods. At first, I kept getting distracted by my thoughts. I was in an obsessive loop arguing with my unreasonable boss in my head. The only relief was my fantasy about leaving the job and getting a new one. Then I realized that I was missing the point of the exercise because I wasn't paying attention to my outer surroundings. Here was all this beautiful nature, and I might as well have been in a mall or a jail cell!

So I made myself look, listen, and smell. It was calming. I noticed that it felt as if I'd come there for the first time, even though I'd walked this path often in the past. I came upon a small patch of moss that attracted me and wondered how long it had been there. Then I saw a couple of caterpillar cocoons. I kept looking at them trying to figure out how they got there, why they were so sticky, and when the new creature might emerge. Suddenly, a huge yellow and red butterfly with exquisite wings appeared out of nowhere and landed on a branch about ten inches from me. I was captivated by its beauty. It looked so vulnerable, but it was also very daring because it came so close to me and stayed there for a long time. I was enthralled.

The butterfly left and returned again a few times before it finally departed for good. I looked at it, the cocoons, and the moss with a growing fascination. I had a million questions! I realize that I must have sat there for nearly an hour, because by the time I got up, it had started to get dark.

You'd said to find the personal-life metaphor, and it was so obvious—it jumped right out at me. Of all the things

I could be looking at in this forest, I was focused on the symbols of transformation: the butterfly and the caterpillar cocoons.

I realized that this is a metaphor for my current life experience. I'm the larva in the cocoon that has almost outgrown my surroundings (my job), and I'm getting ready to be the butterfly. I'm vulnerable but also persistent, and I know how to take risks. The butterfly's willingness to come very close to me was a metaphor for the part of me that's daring to think about expressing my truth; I'm very close to leaving my rut and entering the unknown. But I keep going back to work just as the butterfly returned a few times before it was ready to leave completely.

The moss that originally attracted me symbolizes my need for a soft, nurturing, safe space inside myself to hang out with my dreams for a new life. As I started to walk to my car, I tripped and ran into a prickly bush that scratched my leg. I laughed out loud at the appearance of this metaphor for my boss! Later that night, I got out my paints from the back of the bedroom closet. I hadn't touched them since I began working at my job six years ago. I painted all night. I used every shade of green, yellow, and red, and filled one entire canvas with clusters of sprawling, moist moss. My favorite painting included me wrapped around a fuzzy caterpillar in a large white cocoon. I gave myself long, branchlike arms that extended out of the cocoon and became part of a large pine tree; a yellow and red butterfly sat on my branch. In the corner, I painted an image of me jumping off a diving board into a sea of moss.

Kate told me that story the next week. We laughed and cried as she shared her experience, and we looked at her magnificent paintings. She'd uncorked her curiosity bottle and creativity poured out. For almost a year in our sessions, she'd mentioned that she "used to paint" but felt "creatively blocked." Her blocked creativity and her stuck job seemed like rigid bookends that kept her from reading the next page of her life story. We both recognized that the trip to her closet to rescue her paints represented a major breakthrough.

I asked Kate to imagine herself as a character in a story as well as the writer of her own tale. By engaging her creative process and her powers of curiosity, she gave her inner author permission to discover *what happens next* in her character's life. I'm pleased to tell you that Kate left her stifling job the following month, took a long journey to Greece, and is currently teaching art at a private high school. She paints and writes regularly.

chapter 2

What, Me Creative?

*"It takes courage to grow up and
turn out to be who you really are."*

— e.e. cummings

Over the years, I've asked many people how they view their relationship to creativity. A surprising number shrink back from the idea that they're creative. I remember one woman saying to me, "Well, I crochet, but that's not really creative because I follow patterns." Another man, the founder and CEO of a very successful company, looked me in the eye and said, "I'm not very creative." I nearly fell out of my seat as I thought about his company's impressive track record for innovation.

I flashed on the cartoon of Alfred E. Neuman from *Mad* magazine, smiling gap-toothed with the caption "What, Me Worry?" and it occurred to me that people often hide behind a "What, Me Creative?" persona. Does the prospect of being seen as creative make us worry? And what are we worried about? Are we afraid that we'll end up looking like Alfred if we dare to take an acting class or learn how to sing? A participant in one of my workshops told me that being creative felt terrifying, and another man said it seemed like a burden. One woman insisted that she was "practical, but *not* creative," as if the two were mutually exclusive.

Because I've heard statements like these so often, I've come to realize that the notion of creativity is frequently associated with something difficult or special that other talented people do. Those *real* creative individuals might be the ones who get paid to do it or who call themselves artists by trade. This kind of thinking confuses our professional calling with our innate impulse to explore, develop, and express our imagination. Sadly, it seems that many people feel shy or insecure about their creativity.

I see the creative process as a powerful source of life energy, fulfillment, and personal evolution—a flowing river of impulses. It gives oxygen to your soul and deeper meaning to your life. It's your special way of solving problems, brainstorming new ideas, expressing artistic impulses, or making something beautiful that was missing until you came along. Whatever you imagine, invent, envision, analyze, produce, write, or dream about is part of this process.

Everyone has a creative process, although we often don't give it much thought—we just engage in dozens of creative acts throughout the day. Whether we're devising an alternative route home to avoid a traffic snarl or planning a special meal, we're calling upon our creativity. This drive to conceive and manifest new ideas is basic—I believe it's as vital as the need for food, water, shelter, sex, and relationships. But have we ever heard someone say that they're wearing an inspiration-hormone patch to increase their creativity drive? I doubt it.

How can you make *your* creativity an active, fulfilling, and ongoing part of your life? Stressful, time-cramped modern schedules have an insidious tendency to shortchange your creativity department. But remember the old workout adage: "If you don't use it, you lose it." In the case of creativity, you might say: "If you don't use it *consciously,* you lose it." Creativity is similar to physical fitness: To develop and strengthen your creative process "muscles," you need to practice regularly with clear intention.

Taking a Risk to Play a New Role

We begin as highly imaginative children who play made-up games for hours by devising elaborate fantasies, characters, and plots. But by the time we reach adulthood, many of us feel self-conscious or disconnected from our ability to be creative. Why does this happen? It might be related to the roles we're conditioned to play in our various life journeys. Sometimes when a sibling or other family member excels artistically, the creator role becomes assigned to that person.

Many folks arrive at my improvisation workshops with glowing tales about the extraordinary talent their brothers, sisters, or parents possess. Several years ago, a woman named Arlene joined one of my weekend theater retreats. She walked into the room and introduced herself by saying, "Hi, I'm Arlene. I'm not really sure why I'm here because I'm terrible at this stuff. You should have my sister in your class—*she's* the actor in the family."

At first glance, this might seem like a relatively benign comment. But a closer look revealed the pain and insecurity behind the cheery smile and joking demeanor. Arlene had accepted her role in the family as the "well-meaning caretaker" who always sat in the front row for her sister's performances. In Arlene's mind, the role of creative person was already taken. It was no surprise that she began our meeting by dutifully informing me that she was not the creative one. She was trying to lower my expectations about her abilities, but she was actually introducing herself as a role, rather than as a person. She was basically saying, "Hi, I play the role of non-creative person in my family. How are you?"

Sometimes people see themselves as uncreative simply because they never had the opportunity to cultivate this side of their personality. They might be consumed by a demanding career that leaves little time for other activities, or they may be devoted to raising children. Some moms tell me that they have no time for their own creative pursuits, even though caring for children is a highly creative adventure in improvisation. Each day brings a new surprise or learning opportunity as parents regroup to keep up with their children's inventiveness. Often, tired moms or dads show up at my workshops looking to reclaim their creativity and zest. The first order of business is to help them see themselves as independent, creative adults as they let go of the "I'm just a mom" or "I'm just a dad" role.

Before we can authentically utter the words, "I am creative," we need to have recent positive experiences where we feel validated and excited about our sense of artistry. If we haven't been involved in creative activities since grammar school, it makes sense that our imagination factory might seem like it has a padlock on the front door. On the other hand, some people might say they're not creative because they had an unpleasant encounter in a class or performance.

I worked with a woman who'd been teased and humiliated as a teenager in a tap-dancing class. She told me that she had trouble learning the steps and felt traumatized by the laughter of the other students as she struggled to keep up with the routines. She stopped dancing for many years.

Her path back to creativity involved exorcising those early memories and building her confidence to try improvisational dance. By improvising movement, she could allow the steps and gestures to arise from inside the safety of her own body; she didn't have to match someone else's choreography.

The "What, Me Creative?" persona is often adopted for one more reason: It can be a convenient mask to conceal the sadness or grief we feel if creativity once comprised a major part of our life, but no longer does. I've worked with countless self-described "ex-creators" and "ex-artists" who recount a painful separation from their calling because of illness, injury, family circumstances, financial constraints, inner blocks, or disappointments. After years of exile from their creative identity, they began to mistakenly believe that they'd lost their gifts forever. Reclaiming their abilities means breaking out of a role they may not be aware they're playing, such as "The former talent who's all washed-up" or "The promising genius who's now a has-been." Although reconnecting with dreams may seem impossible or overwhelming, it's never too late to turn over a fresh page and begin again.

The good news is that although you may lose touch with the original lifespring of your creative self, the rediscovery process can be exquisitely satisfying and simple. The first step is to do what you're doing right now by reading this book— that is, make room in your busy day to contemplate your particular strengths and interests as a creative person. Do you have a creative outlet you'd like to develop more seriously, or is there a new direction you'd like to explore? What are your natural gifts? What crafts or art forms attract you—what stirs your passion and tickles your imagination? Would you like to get back to a practice you haven't done for years? What role did you play in your family and how does it influence your relationship to creativity?

23

Problem-Solve, Design, Invent, and Express

After setting aside some time for yourself, it's useful to consider which aspect of the creative process best reflects your present inclinations. I've found that there are at least four major aspects.

1. First, there's a need for ingenuity to overcome an obstacle or figure out a puzzle. This is the **problem-solver** aspect of creativity where you're looking for solutions or answers. Have you ever set off on a camping trip only to realize that you forgot the silverware? You might have noticed hungry hikers huddled around a propane stove eagerly offering their makeshift devices to help scoop up piping hot soup! Maybe you've tried to find a constructive tactic to give a co-worker feedback about a behavior that's annoying you. Whether you're discovering substitute spoons or strategizing about how to be effective in your communication, you're exercising the problem-solver muscles of the creative process.

2. The second aspect of creativity, the **designer,** is embodied in your desire to bring harmony and beauty to your environment and yourself. When this part of your being is active, you might feel compelled to refinish a piece of furniture, try a new style of clothing, or invite a feng shui expert to give advice about your kitchen. The designer aspect looks at everyday surroundings as a creative canvas. The impulse to design is linked to your need to make conscious decisions about the shapes, symmetry, colors, forms, and patterns that you choose for the settings you inhabit, as well as the clothing you wear.

3. The **inventor** dimension of creativity propels you to add something new to the world. This aspect is born from your curiosity—in other words, there's a little bit of Thomas Edison in everybody! The inventor seeks to nurture great ideas and translate them into new accomplishments. The qualities of enthusiasm, vision, and practicality are key to any innovation. It might show up as a new game you create to entertain bored children at a family gathering, or you might get inspired to invent a new gardening tool or computer program. I know a man who's devising an interactive Website using his poetry and paintings.

4. The fourth aspect of creativity is the **expresser**—the urge to convey your thoughts, feelings, musings, and imagination. You might want to sing a song, write a short story, create a dance, or weave a rug. This dimension of your creative spirit longs to share what's inside you with others, because self-expression is crucial for the realization of your fullest potential. When you cultivate the expresser aspect, you're daring to share your unique perception of the world, and you're also giving shape and form to a vision that deserves to be communicated. This part of you develops your ability to be seen and heard and is an essential ingredient for networking and building community. Giving your expresser an outlet builds confidence and strengthens the bonds of relationship with others.

As you look at your creative process, you might find it helpful to consider which of these aspects most reflects your current yearnings. Is the problem-solver motivating you by tickling your thought process to find solutions to a puzzling question or obstacle? Or do you find yourself looking around your home or office with a designer's eye that might be coaxing you to bring more beauty to your surroundings? Perhaps your inner inventor is looking for a way to make something new. Is the expresser facet of your process nudging you to find a creative vehicle for your innermost stirrings? Do you want to express this impulse with words, images, music, or textures?

Do you tend to exercise your creativity through all of these aspects, or do you gravitate toward just one or two of them? Try practicing the one that you avoid in order to strengthen your confidence and aptitude in that area. You might rediscover an innate talent by daring to apply an aspect of creativity that you haven't used for a while. For example, if you notice that you're inclined to choose activities that usually involve problem-solving, you might challenge yourself to exercise your expresser mode.

Versatility is an indispensable asset in creativity. The goal is to become skillful in each of these aspects so that you can adapt to a variety of challenges. I know a choreographer who sparked a revival of her creative process by remodeling and redesigning her barn. She transformed a dilapidated old building into a sunny rehearsal studio with gleaming wood floors. Tearing down walls, measuring plywood, and banging nails provided an unforeseen impetus for her fallow artistic period, as her problem-solver and designer aspects awakened her expresser dimension. As soon as she finished the barn, she was motivated to begin work on an exciting new dance piece that she humorously called *Demolition Duets.* Her reconnection with her creative process had been stimulated by the use of her toolbox instead of her ballet slippers!

ROCK ART BIRTH

chapter 3

Reclaiming Your Creative Self

"And the day came when the risk to remain tight in a bud was more painful than the risk it took to blossom."

— Anaïs Nin

I'm convinced that the repression of creativity underlies many problems in our world. When creativity is blocked because of inner wounds or outer oppression, pain and frustration result. We feel hopeless and purposeless as our instinctive needs to create and imagine become subverted into destructive (or self-destructive) reactions. The inability to express ourselves as full human beings is a deep source of alienation. We need to make contact with our creative spirit, but we often don't know how or we may not feel that we have the right to give it much time.

Sometimes we're afraid of what might come out of our unconscious if we open these channels: We fear that people will think we're crazy, boring, offensive, silly, or unoriginal. So we clam up and play it safe. Meanwhile, there's a nagging void and uneasiness as we try to move through our lives like robots. We pay a big price for ignoring our creative impulses.

Have you ever felt that your creativity was straying away from you like a child who gets lost in a department store? You start out holding the hand of your creative self with an inner promise to make space in your hectic week for that special project you love. You resolve to write, dance, sing, knit, play the guitar, photograph nature, or paint—you might even prepare by collecting all the materials you need. The next thing you know, your boss plops something urgent on your desk, your daughter wakes up with chicken pox, or a friend comes into town unexpectedly.

A few weeks later you emerge from a haze of hyperactivity with a nagging feeling that you've forgotten something. What *was* that thing you were going to do? You might feel restless, guilty, or bothered. Suddenly, as if from a distance, you hear your scratchy inner sound system announcing: *There's a lost creative self wandering around by the checkout line. Would someone please come and claim it?* It doesn't take long before you realize that you've lost touch with your creative intention.

Sound familiar? Once again the hard-core urgencies of life succeeded in trumping your "softer" creativity goals. Carburetor repairs take priority over calligraphy class. Parent-teacher meetings cancel singing practice. Food shopping trumps writing your memoirs, and buying a present for your sister's baby shower edges out painting with watercolors. On one level this sounds entirely reasonable, so why question it? Of course your basic family and work responsibilities come first. Food, shelter, homework done on time, having the right dress for a wedding—these are the necessities of life, right? And while we're on the subject, have you cleaned your refrigerator, organized your sock drawer, and scrubbed the toilet?

You might hear a similar refrain in your head each time you dare to entertain the possibility of taking some time for your creative process. I call this inner voice the "drill sergeant" who commands you to work, work, work! This relentless taskmaster views creativity as frivolous and implores you to spend every waking moment crossing things off an endless to-do list. The remedy? Ask your drill sergeant for a time-out from your list while you give yourself periods of *creative free time* during your day or week.

You might hear some objections or grumbling from your drill sergeant, but I guarantee that these will soon fade into the background as you begin to notice that creative pursuits actually revitalize your energy. You'll probably have more motivation to get things done after you spend a couple of hours being creative. Your drill sergeant will be thrilled to discover that these sessions make your to-do lists seem less daunting— self-expression is a definite vim-and-vigor boost.

Creative Free Time

This is a period that you set aside for nurturing and stimulating your creative imagination, and it's important to establish clear boundaries by adding it to your appointment book. In the beginning, you might want to ask friends or family members to help you keep the time sacred and uninterrupted. Think of these sessions as gifts to yourself. You have the delicious freedom to do whatever inspires you in order to get your creative juices flowing, and you're courting the natural rhythms of your creative process through the two steps of preparation and stimulation.

Preparation

The first step is to get ready. If your mind is filled with lots of details from home or work life, you might begin by meditating, taking a bath, practicing yoga, or sipping tea in the garden. Before you can begin, you need to *get ready* to begin. By choosing to do activities that are refreshing, revitalizing, and relaxing, you're sending a message to your creative mind that says: "I'm here and I'm open to receiving inspiration." You're giving yourself the freedom to till the soil of your imagination without being distracted by anybody else's needs or expectations.

In the beginning you may desire a tall glass of daydreaming with a twist of creativity. In this quiet, reflective mode, you're clearing away your mental clutter and making room for the present moment. You're opening your mind in a sense.

This preparation is the important emptying phase of your creative process. You might enjoy journaling about your next creative endeavor or reading a book or article that relates to your artistic interests. If you have a longer period of time, you might begin with stretching, walking, getting a massage, or doing another enjoyable activity (such as dancing to your favorite music).

The key is to realize that you're not wasting time by doing these kinds of warm-ups. You'll find that you have greater energy and motivation after you take the time to empty your mind and prepare for creative expression. As Gertrude Stein said, "It takes a lot of time to be a genius, you have to sit around so much doing nothing, really doing nothing."

Stimulation

The next step is to stimulate your right brain by engaging your nonlinear thinking. Choose a creative activity that you enjoy: Draw a sketch of the scenery in your backyard, explore rhythms with a hand drum, or make colorful jewelry. Another wonderful way to cultivate your intuitive artistic awareness is to go on a photography walk where you take photos of random objects, places, and people that catch your eye. You can transform ordinary items and locations in your neighborhood into extraordinary images by experimenting with perspective and composition. A close-up of a wooden gatepost or a bicycle wheel might yield a fascinating shot, or you might choose to focus on composition by capturing a gang of pigeons standing around a college student's laptop in the park. By exploring these kinds of activities, you're preparing your body and mind for a creative experience by arousing your artistic sensibilities.

Creativity involves taking a risk to try something new by breaking out of your habitual patterns of perception and response. As you transcend the predictable structure of your logical thinking, you're inviting a spirit of discovery and adventure. Making art is an act of defiance—you're defying a lifetime of conditioning that grooms you to play it safe instead of thinking outside the box. You're also standing up to inner demons who say, *No, you can't,* and *If you try, you'll fail.* You're daring to venture beyond the comfort of the known in order to be surprised by the challenge of the unknown as you search for new ways of seeing, hearing, and shaping the world around you.

If you already have an ongoing creative project, use your creative free time to gather new ideas and make notes about the direction of your next steps. Give yourself an opportunity to brainstorm and play with themes. What are your goals for this project? How would you like to approach it, and what resources will you need? What excites you about this idea? What would you like to express or create? What skills do you need to acquire?

The more space you carve out of your day or week for creative pursuits, the more facility you'll develop. Mastery comes with practice, and committing regularly to some creative free time brings perceptible development to your creative process. Eventually, you'll find that you want more time for gathering resources and experimenting. Try to schedule some open-ended chunks of time so that you can sink your teeth into your project, make some headway, and hone your skills.

Inspire Yourself Regularly

Creative free time is also an opportunity to invite inspiration. The activities of everyday life don't foster an inspired state of mind; dullness can easily set in as we go through the routines of our day. Inspiration begins by simply reconnecting with our breath. The expression "catch my breath" is very revealing: Like our creative process, our breath does seem to "run away" from us on a regular basis. We need to track it down, assess its condition, and release it from the clutches of life's stressful holding patterns. Sometimes this begins with a simple internal awareness: *Oops, I'm holding my breath again!*

Have you ever decided to become conscious of your breath, only to realize that you're barely breathing at all? Maybe a perceptive friend or therapist noticed you were holding your breath while talking about a difficult subject. The creative process requires fullness of breath, and it's no accident that the in-breath is called "inspiration." The most fundamental act of creativity is happening hundreds of times every hour, and it's called "breathing"! On a cellular level, every breath sustains new growth by delivering oxygen to our blood, which in turn nourishes our body.

There's a direct correlation between our productivity or output and the time we devote to rejuvenation or input. If we become hyperfocused on *out*come, our *in*come may suffer in more ways than one. Our inhalation needs to be as deep and complete as our exhalation, but often we're pulling in more air without fully releasing what's in our lungs. Our in-breath may be too shallow. A balanced breath gives us the inspiration we need to keep our imagination open and active, and our powers of creativity are strongest when our breathing is full and unhampered.

Conscious breathing also supports you to find the motivation to manifest your creative impulses. Try working with your breath as a technique for *inspiring yourself* when you're beginning a creative project or feeling blocked. Take a few moments to sit quietly and practice breathing slowly, with complete in-breaths and out-breaths. Imagine that each inhalation brings fuel for your imagination, as well as your body. Use your exhalation as a vehicle to allow stale air and old thought patterns to expire. Let go of what you don't need, and press the "refresh" button to clear a new page in your mind.

Physical and Creative Movement

If you're looking for positive results in your creative expression, physical exercise is crucial. The health benefits of exercise are indisputable: lower blood pressure; increased strength, flexibility, brain vitality, and cardiovascular fitness; and a stronger immune system. But did you realize that a stuck body and a stuck creative process often go hand in hand? As you release pent-up physical stress, you also increase your ability to express thoughts, feelings, and ideas. When people tell me that they feel creatively blocked or uninspired, I always begin by suggesting ongoing physical workouts or dance. The body-mind connection is a major component of the creative process, so be sure to include exercise in your week.

The combination of regular exercise and creative expression also enhances mental acuity and memory. Later in the book, Wren discusses how knitting can contribute to your brain's well-being. Medical studies are now showing that learning new skills, solving puzzles, and deciphering unfamiliar information keeps your brain healthy and active. These kinds of tasks may even delay the development of various neurological memory disorders. A famous study at the Salk Institute for Biological Studies in California focused on the role of exercise in brain development. Rodents (who happen to love to exercise) were divided into two groups: One set was given lots of opportunity to run on exercise wheels, while the other group was prevented from engaging in physical activity. The results were stunning: The rodents who exercised increased the number of neurons in their hippocampus (the part of the brain where information is encoded into new memory), but the sedentary rodents didn't. These neurons may be essential for learning, creativity, and improved memory function. So the next time you're on the treadmill or elliptical machine feeling a little bored, think about all those groovy neurons you're making!

SHADOW PLAY

chapter 4

The Psychological Stages of the Creative Process

"What a strange machine man is! . . . You fill him with bread, wine, fish, radishes, and out of him come sighs, laughter and dreams."

— Nikos Kazantzakis

While each person has a unique experience with the creative process, there are some feelings and states of mind that everyone goes through. As you create, it's helpful to view your particular journey in the context of these universal stages. You can gain tremendous insight about where you are in the process, what experiences you might encounter, how you tend to get stuck (and unstuck), and what helps you succeed. Creativity is a journey of investigation, change, and refinement. As your initial idea grows and changes, *you, too,* are changing and evolving.

Mastery in the creative process depends on the cultivation of two sets of skills: First, you need to acquire *proficiency* in the techniques of your art or craft; and second, you need to develop *emotional dexterity* to help you navigate through the various psychological states that are likely to arise. Great artistic technique can be squandered if it isn't accompanied by a savvy awareness of the *psychology of creativity.*

Let's look at some common psychological stages that often arise during the creative process. You might recognize many of these states of mind, although I find that they're not necessarily linear—you may discover that you skip some stages or experience them in a different order. There may also be occasions when your creative project evokes a different progression of feelings. However, these are some common experiences:

◇◇◇◇◇◇◇◇◇◇◇◇◇◇◇◇◇◇◇◇◇◇◇◇◇◇◇◇◇◇◇◇◇◇

The Itch: This is the preconscious inner rumbling that tells us a creative impulse is trying to come to the surface. Ideas are brewing, and we feel a bit distracted while doing other tasks; images are scratching at the corners of our minds, hoping to get our attention. Nothing is formed yet, but there's a pulsing sense of "something coming." We feel fidgety, restless, expectant, a bit anxious, and curious.

◇◇◇◇◇◇◇◇◇◇◇◇◇◇◇◇◇◇◇◇◇◇◇◇◇◇◇◇◇◇◇◇◇◇

The Wow: A flash of inspiration stirs our imagination, and we're thrilled by a fabulous vision. We hear or envision it—whatever *it* is! It could be a book concept, a song, a home-remodeling design, a character monologue, a strategic business plan, a screenplay idea, or a garden-landscaping plan. We're possessed with a passionate sense of purpose, on a mission that promises great possibilities. We're flying high in the rarefied air of discovery and invention. We feel joyful, stimulated, excited, optimistic, passionate, buoyant, positive, motivated, and uplifted.

◇◇◇◇◇◇◇◇◇◇◇◇◇◇◇◇◇◇◇◇◇◇◇◇◇◇◇◇◇◇◇◇◇◇◇◇

The Flood: A torrent of impulses, ideas, words, images, sounds, movements, shapes, or designs burst forth like a giant tsunami. We're in the flow, the waters of creation are gushing, and we're riding atop the waves, naked and exhilarated. We feel as if we can't get the ideas out fast enough—there's so much to express! We have to buy food or go to sleep, but we don't want to stop what we're doing. We're riding the river rapids in a seemingly limitless deluge of ideas. We feel fertile, wet, hopeful, loving, open, generous, juicy, and alive.

◇◇◇◇◇◇◇◇◇◇◇◇◇◇◇◇◇◇◇◇◇◇◇◇◇◇◇◇◇◇◇◇◇◇◇◇

The Quest: We want to set off on an adventure to learn *everything* we can find that illuminates our new subject. A strong desire to research and explore arises. Like a detective, we're looking for clues, leads, and connecting information that will boost our initial hunches. We're hungry for more background material and titillated by the prospect of discovering new insights. We want to investigate whatever resources might help our creative project grow and flourish. The hunt is on—and the intellectual search hounds are running! We feel obsessed, intrigued, consumed, inquisitive, aroused, and hungry for knowledge.

◇◇◇◇◇◇◇◇◇◇◇◇◇◇◇◇◇◇◇◇◇◇◇◇◇◇◇◇◇◇◇◇◇◇◇◇

The Marinating: It's time to let all the ideas and information soak in the marinade of our imagination. We feel inclined to take the creative-alchemy pot off the front burner so that it can cook more slowly. We want to let the new concept settle and steep in the creative juices of our unconscious. We might say we want to "sleep on it," or we might prefer to go through the day with our project simmering in the back of our minds. We feel quiet, calm, satisfied, eager to take a break, and maybe a bit tired.

◇◇◇◇◇◇◇◇◇◇◇◇◇◇◇◇◇◇◇◇◇◇◇◇◇◇◇◇◇◇◇◇◇

The Dock: We begin to feel the need to "ground" our ideas. We need an outline, an overview, a character sketch, a rough drawing, or a chord progression. We want to bring our juicy, wet ideas onto dry land and need the earth element to make us feel solid about our inspiration. We want to bring the creative impulses down into the realm of matter by giving them form and shape. We have a strong desire to be practical, logical, responsible, thoughtful, and specific. We feel determined, focused, and a bit agitated as we try to create a working structure or container for our vision.

◇◇◇◇◇◇◇◇◇◇◇◇◇◇◇◇◇◇◇◇◇◇◇◇◇◇◇◇◇◇◇◇◇

The Laboratory: We aren't satisfied with the docking efforts so far. The structure isn't working, and the renderings fall short of our expectations. We're still swimming in ideas, searching for land, but we need to experiment with some new approaches. We pull out the Bunsen burner and flasks of solutions and get busy trying to solidify a fluid, mercurial concept. We're dedicated to solving the problem. We feel challenged, perplexed, open-minded, driven, uncertain, uneasy, and a little worried.

◇◇◇◇◇◇◇◇◇◇◇◇◇◇◇◇◇◇◇◇◇◇◇◇◇◇◇◇◇◇◇◇◇

The Thwarting: Suddenly, a troublesome, unexpected external circumstance intrudes into our process. This outer obstacle presents itself like an irksome, uninvited houseguest who throws a monkey wrench into our plans. It's a curveball that might take the form of a contentious interaction with an important collaborator, or it might show up as a logistical nightmare. We feel stumbling blocks are being thrown in our path by the gods of disruption: A blizzard arrives on opening night, the frame shop loses an original print, or the computer crashes in the middle of writing our best chapter. This outer thwarting triggers an internal conflict that further complicates our process. We consider launching a campaign in Congress to repeal Murphy's Law, or becoming a recluse at the nearest hermitage. We feel anxious, exasperated, stymied, explosive, and victimized.

$$\diamondsuit$$

The Deflation: We begin thinking, *Oh no, this is going to be harder than we thought!* The laboratory is cluttered with empty flasks, and the Bunsen burner has run out of gas. We've ripped up ten false starts of outlines, and the pad of drawing paper is empty because all the pages are in the trash. Nothing feels right. Every grounded container we try to create for our grand inspiration seems paltry, insufficient, mundane, inadequate, inappropriate, or stupid. We can't seem to bring the spirit of our inspiration into matter. The fizz is gone, and there's a queasy sense of dissolution. We're searching for an elegant material home for a beautiful, pure spirit, but nothing fits. We feel sad, frustrated, crestfallen, disillusioned, discouraged, irritated, anxious, deflated, and disappointed.

$$\diamondsuit$$

The Wall: The deflation turns into a flat, cold, impenetrable obstacle of impossibility. We feel stuck, blocked, and we can't move forward. We're in a crisis. All of our ideas seem boring, tired, old, used, and hackneyed. We seem to be trapped in a horror film, wondering, *How did we get here? Weren't we just flying high with positive enthusiasm? Why did we start this whole thing? We could be somewhere else having fun.* The wall is closing in, and we feel claustrophobic. We can't breathe. The wall is formidable and insurmountable. Worst of all, it seems merciless in its refusal to give us an inch of progress. We feel depressed, scared, humiliated, defeated, duped, hopeless, powerless, weak, insecure, ineffectual, and vulnerable.

◇◇◇◇◇◇◇◇◇◇◇◇◇◇◇◇◇◇◇◇◇◇◇◇◇◇◇◇◇◇◇◇◇◇◇

The Rebellion: We decide to forget the whole thing. *The hell with it—we won't let this stupid creative idea ruin our lives.* We might as well toss it into the trash. Who cares if we're throwing the baby out with the bathwater? We pitch the tea over the side of the boat as we proclaim our mutiny in the face of this oppressive and controlling project. Who cares if we're mixing metaphors? Viva la revolución! We'll no longer be taxed by the drudgery of this dreadful chore. We resolve to abandon the project, refusing to submit to the pain, agony, discomfort, and torture of the creative process for even one more second. We'll go back to being mindless blobs watching TV. We feel desperate, angry, defiant, insolent, disobedient, bold, free, oppositional, and relieved.

◇◇◇◇◇◇◇◇◇◇◇◇◇◇◇◇◇◇◇◇◇◇◇◇◇◇◇◇◇◇◇◇◇◇◇

The Denial: We pretend that everything's just fine and nothing's bothering us. We don't miss being in the creative process. We're actually so happy to have the time to organize the paper clips and alphabetize the spices. We think, *Phew! What a relief!* but deep inside we feel like a failure. We've let someone down, but we don't want to think about *who* it might be. We miss our pal, the muse of creativity, but we won't admit it to anyone, least of all ourselves. We feel numb, defensive, edgy, guilty, depressed, and lonely. Most of the time, though, we're not feeling much of anything.

◇◇◇◇◇◇◇◇◇◇◇◇◇◇◇◇◇◇◇◇◇◇◇◇◇◇◇◇◇◇◇◇

The Wake: The denial layer cracks open, and the full weight of the loss hits us. We can finally feel how much we miss being involved in the creative process: *Ouch!* We experience unbearable pain and feel very heavy. We're in mourning. Our creative project is now reduced to ashes that lifelessly inhabit an urn on the mantelpiece. We welcome visitors who come to pay their last respects and sit shivah. Our inner characters offer condolences: Our juicy self comes to say how sad it is to be dry and brittle, our hopeful self comes to plead with us to try again, our grounded self apologizes for letting us down and promises to do better next time, our guilty self takes all the blame for this terrible tragedy . . . and our original inspiration comes to tell us unequivocally that *it's not dead.* We hear the comforting messages from a distance, but they don't matter. We're inconsolable. None of these well-wishers can break through the dead zone where we're trapped. We feel a deep kinship with Vincent van Gogh—we consider removing an ear or maybe a nose. Although we miss the dance with creativity, we don't dare imagine starting up again. We feel sad, pained, miserable, anguished, and lost. We're experiencing tremendous grief.

◇◇◇◇◇◇◇◇◇◇◇◇◇◇◇◇◇◇◇◇◇◇◇◇◇◇◇◇◇◇◇◇

The Glimmer: We begin to feel the shadow of a hint of the itch again. While we're mourning, we wander into the empty creative room down the hall, where we haven't been since the death of our project. We decide to sneak in and pack up some of the images, writings, and renderings. Immediately and unexpectedly, we feel completely at home. *Wait a minute—this isn't as bad as I thought.* We're pleasantly surprised to see that some of what we'd started earlier is really quite good, but we don't want to get too optimistic. We're guarded and skeptical. We're also playing hard to get: *If this creative idea wants to play again, it will have to give me something more than it gave me last time.* Secretly, we realize that *we* will have to give something more, too. But we don't want to be disappointed again, so we're playing our cards close to our chest. We want to have a sober look around to see if there's any life left in what we abandoned. We experience subtle stirrings. We feel subdued excitement, cautious arousal, and muted hopefulness.

◇◇◇◇◇◇◇◇◇◇◇◇◇◇◇◇◇◇◇◇◇◇◇◇◇◇◇◇◇◇◇◇

The Testing: We make a private bargain: *Okay, I'll try again, but only until it begins to feel frustrating.* We're half invested and say that we don't really care one way or the other now. We'll just do it for the hell of it, for the fun of it. We have nothing to lose. The wake has already happened, and our worst fears of failure have already occurred and reduced us to humble earthlings. Our puffed-up, inflated, grandiose ego has been popped, and now we're simply human. Our starry-eyed, naïve dreams of nirvana had cold water thrown on them, so we figure that we can dip our toes into the water with no pressure to be perfect. Okay, so we might not get a Pulitzer Prize or an Academy Award for this project. It will be a little experiment, a test. We'll see what happens: Can we manage to make this fun and meaningful at the same time? We decide to give it a try. We feel relieved, released, open, curious, moved, and a little excited.

The Reunion: The testing gives way to an unexpected meeting with our creative self. We love what we see! Like old friends who haven't seen each other for years, the dialogue picks up effortlessly where it left off without skipping a beat. We may find the original inspiration, which might be the same, or we may find an entirely new approach. Either way, we're thrilled to run into the arms of creativity. *Yippee!* We rediscover the tension of the creative tango again, the give and take. We're back in the flow, and the ideas are streaming. We're itching to jump in and make something beautiful. We feel ecstatic, liberated, and hopeful again.

The Lovemaking: We're creating! The passion is rekindled, and we've fallen in love again. Everywhere we look we see the face of our creative project. Everything around us suddenly becomes a source of creative stimulation. We feel giddy, yet grounded. Our innocence has matured, as our naïve expectations of instant success have been replaced with wisdom and patience. We're making a baby! We're ready to meet the challenges with an intelligent awareness of potential pitfalls. We feel happy, inspired, awakened, stimulated, grateful, and eager.

◇◇◇◇◇◇◇◇◇◇◇◇◇◇◇◇◇◇◇◇◇◇◇◇◇◇◇◇◇◇◇◇◇

The Pruning: Now that we've reconnected with our creative passion, we look around and see fragments of the project's previous incarnation. We feel compelled to do some housecleaning since these old remnants are getting in the way of new impulses. We have a strong urge to get rid of everything that doesn't work; all the dead-end ideas have to go. This is the time for chopping and cutting. The lovemaking brought us back to the essence of the core idea, and we want to remove all the "fat" by exercising a discerning eye. We feel confident, clear, motivated, strategic, and unconstrained.

◇◇◇◇◇◇◇◇◇◇◇◇◇◇◇◇◇◇◇◇◇◇◇◇◇◇◇◇◇◇◇◇◇

The Resolve: Nothing will stop us now! In the back of our minds, we know that we'll probably hit that wall again. There will most likely be another rebellion or two, and we have a sense that we might even attend another creativity wake along the way. But this time, we have the advantage of having traveled this territory before. We've learned that there's a way out of the apparent darkness and sense of impossibility. We don't have a perfect map because each visit to one of these psychological stages is always different. The terrain in and out of each state is never exactly the same, but the more we create, the more reliable our compass becomes as we learn to find true north. We feel centered and purposeful.

Think about your creative process and reflect upon the ups and downs of your journey. Do you remember having feelings, thoughts, or challenges that resemble these psychological stages? Look for recurring emotional experiences or states of mind that seem to show up frequently as you create. What states of mind do you tend to go through when you're creating? Can you imagine "making friends" with these feelings? What might help you understand, anticipate, and accept the stages of your process? Can you trace these emotions to earlier experiences in your life? What are the roots of your reactions and thoughts?

Would you like to change your process in any way? What might assist you in making changes? Sometimes it helps to look for humor as you examine the progression of your responses, so try envisioning the psychological stages of your creative process as a cartoon. I find that bringing a touch of absurdity to this exercise is invaluable and liberating.

For example, when I encounter the misery of the wake stage as I'm creating a new theater performance, I imagine myself as a professional mourner who's dressed in black lace from head to toe. I see myself standing at the edge of the grave of my brilliant creative ideas. An imaginary camera comes in for a close-up to catch me wailing, "Why me?" with arms outstretched to the heavens. The cartoon continues until I try to throw myself into the grave while singing an aria from *La Bohème.* Thankfully, my creative project always springs up from the casket just in time to prevent my leap. We run into each other's arms as I transition to the glimmer, testing, and reunion stages of my process. What's your cartoon?

STEPS

chapter 5

Learning Your Creative Work Cycles

*"To everything there is a season and a
time for every purpose under heaven."*

— Ecclesiastes

Once you have a better understanding of the psychological stages of creativity, the next step is getting to know your natural rhythms and work cycles. Your final outcome will be greatly enhanced if you pay attention to the needs of your particular process. Just as the waves of the sea ebb and flow, your creative process has its own organic cycles of productivity and rest.

There's an in-breath and an out-breath in every creative endeavor. The in-breath phase includes receptive activities such as observing, listening, learning, contemplating, gathering, and assimilating. These parts of your work rhythms give you the opportunity to get new inspiration and recharge your batteries. The out-breath phase involves action-oriented pursuits, including implementing, experimenting, editing, problem solving, and manifesting. The action mode satisfies your need for expression, tangible results, and achievements.

Let's take a look at some important work cycles in the creative process:

- Preparation: making time and space for a creative experience

- Inspiration: opening the channels for new ideas to flow in

- Envisioning: free associating, brainstorming, and clarifying the vision

- Exploring and gathering: researching and collecting information or materials

- Contemplation and observation: noticing patterns or themes in your work

- Experimentation: testing your concepts and trying different approaches

- Grappling: navigating through obstacles, doubts, or crises; problem solving

- Cross-fertilizing: bringing fresh inspiration from unrelated activities

- Rediscovery: revisiting and reorganizing the goals or methods of your project

- Digestion and assimilation: integrating what you've learned and discovered

- Filtering: making choices and editing

- Manifestation: making your ideas a concrete reality; executing the plan or vision

Discovering the Fabric of Your Creativity

Understanding and identifying these essential phases in *your* process helps you maintain a steady, motivated creative practice that's undaunted by the shifting tides of your psychological experience. This understanding involves keen inner listening that helps you become more equipped to anticipate and deal with obstacles as they arise. Learning the terrain of your creative process gives you the wisdom and skills you need to succeed. You're discovering the *fabric of your creativity.*

Timing is everything. Knowing where you are in your project's developmental continuum is crucial. On a certain day you might have a strong desire to investigate and research, while some moments urge you to invite more inspiration. On other days you might feel compelled to roll up your sleeves, work energetically, and produce results. At times you may find yourself in a reflective mode, needing to contemplate your next steps, or you may hear your creative process begging for space to digest and assimilate what you've done so far. Still other periods are best spent exploring new concepts.

The key is to *listen* to the call of your creative self and join with the impulse that seems to be emerging. *One of the most difficult and frustrating mistakes people make while creating is pushing themselves to be in a cycle that conflicts with their natural inclination that day.* This tendency can be a prescription for disaster because it puts you in a power struggle with your own instincts. Remember, creativity is a *process,* not just the final outcome—and every cycle is important. Which one are you currently experiencing? Are you in an in-breath or out-breath phase at this point in your project's development?

Observing What Matters

I coached a woman named Sandy who chronically re-sisted the contemplative phase of her creative process. She felt she was "wasting time" if she wasn't doing, doing, doing every moment. She'd mercilessly push herself to "accomplish something" and beat herself up when she had a less produc-tive day. She worked very hard and couldn't understand why she wasn't making more progress.

Sandy is a retired teacher and a devoted clay artist. Her complaint was that each morning she'd begin with a feeling of dissatisfaction as she looked at her pieces from the previ-ous day. When I met her, she'd been trying to master a new technique for overglazing, but she was frustrated by what she called her "fiascos and flops." Her solution was to trash the previous day's efforts and start over.

I suggested that she might want to spend some time observing and studying her pieces instead of throwing them away. My intuition told me that the answer to her problem would emerge from quiet observation and contemplation, which would also give her an opportunity to track her prog-ress. She insisted that wasn't necessary, however, and felt im-patient with the idea of "not doing anything." She wanted to charge forward with her next attempt to solve the problem.

I mentioned that it seemed she was blocking her creative in-breath by hurling herself into action without the benefit of reflection. I asked her to imagine going through the day with only exhalations and no inhalations. She got a little irritated and said that she didn't think the metaphor applied to her. But to her credit, she decided to try my suggestions anyway, so I invited her to retrieve her "failed" vessels from the trash and simply sit in front of them. I asked her to suspend her thinking and contemplate the various forms without doing

TIMELESS VESSEL

anything to fix them. I encouraged her to let the clay pieces "speak" to her about what they needed. After 20 minutes, I asked her to write about her observations in her journal.

To her surprise (and mine) she wrote that the clay felt "scared" and needed her to move more slowly and carefully as she handled it. She needed to make friends with the clay before she could make it behave in a certain way. Her vessel also told her that she needed to check the temperature device in her kiln to be sure it was accurate. Her writing helped her recognize that *she* was scared about overcoming her challenges with overglazing.

Sandy eventually realized that in her rush to "get it right," she'd overlooked a faulty gauge that was allowing the temperature to go too high. She learned that firing the overglaze decoration needs to be done at a lower temperature than the glaze firing. The clay had "spoken," and led her to the remedy for her problem.

I recommended that she incorporate contemplation and observation into her creative process every day, and we continued to do similar practices during our sessions together. A few months later, a beautiful little ochre vessel entitled *In-Breath* arrived at my mailbox with a note that said: "Thanks for reminding me to lower the heat of my expectations and see what's important!"

Listening to Your Moments

Creativity is like gardening. You prepare the earth, till the soil, dig the holes, plant the seeds, water the plants, fertilize the ground, prune the weeds, and eventually enjoy the flowers or harvest the vegetables. Your creative process has similar cycles: Sometimes you have to concentrate on preparing your space, organizing your materials, or gathering your resources; on other days, you need to grab your creative shovel and dig deep. Your imagination may feel hard and frozen on some occasions, so you have to know when to get out the pitchfork and when to melt the frozen ground with the warm waters of acceptance. This awareness comes from *listening* to the needs of your creative cycle.

There will be times when you need to plant seeds of thought and nurture them until they sprout. It's important to know when to let go and when to keep digging. If you keep digging in your garden after you've planted the seeds, you'll prevent them from settling in and growing roots. Some days are all about raking the leaves and pruning the bushes: You need to edit what you've written, clean up your loose ends of yarn, chip away at some rough edges on your sculpture, or sort out the earlier drafts of your musical composition. And don't forget the importance of watering your creative plant as it matures and develops. This might include giving yourself some kudos for your work or asking members of your creative-support community to "water" your creation with their feedback and appreciation.

What are your creative work rituals? Which cycles do you tend to resist or forget to give yourself? In which cycles are you most at home, and which ones are less familiar? Do you listen to the need of your moment? Is there balance in the amount of time you spend on the various tasks of your creative gardening?

As you make a relationship with your creative process by settling into a regular practice, you'll notice that your satisfaction increases when you stay in tune with your deeper impulses. For example, you may have a desire to get up and have a piece of cake after working for ten minutes. Usually, this is an obvious opportunity to test your resolve and strengthen the discipline of your work habits by staying focused on your project, so you decide to resist that impulse because you know it will be a distraction you'll regret later. But if you listen more deeply, you may find that beneath the "Let's go get cake" urge, there's a deeper calling to "sweeten" your experience by reconnecting to the joy of your original vision. While the cake would be nice, what you really need is an injection of excitement or energy. You might find it helpful to talk about your creation with close friends who feel enthusiastic about your work.

෴

Have you ever been in an unproductive period of relentlessly "chewing the bone"? I'm sure you know those days when you've sucked the creative bone dry, but you're still obsessively gnawing at it. It may be time to walk away, clear the slate, and allow the potential for *cross-fertilizing* to happen. Cross-fertilizing occurs when you leave your creative pursuit and do something else that's unrelated. It's like bringing some rich, new loam from another location into your garden. Exercising, going to a museum, catching a movie, taking a shower, playing sports, cooking a meal, sweeping the floor, listening to music, painting a fence, or dancing are all excellent candidates. I find that some of my best ideas arrive after I go hiking.

Remember that having fun definitely oils the wheels of creativity, so don't forget to include playtime. Have you ever noticed that after a day of fun you suddenly have a new perspective on an old problem? Maybe the musical-chord progression that you've been laboring over falls into place with a flash of clarity, or you might envision a new adaptation for a sock-knitting pattern that's been frustrating you. At least one person I know gets ready for his next architectural design by going swing dancing first. Fun primes your creative pump.

On the other hand, if your concentration and energy are yielding productive results, keep going—this is no time for a break! You can always go to the movies tomorrow. The key is to listen to the true need of the moment. As you commit to making creativity a regular aspect of your life, you'll notice that it becomes a steady, reliable refuge that beckons you to return again and again. Wild horses won't be able to keep you away from your special time to dive into your creative process and pursue your latest ideas.

MOMENT

chapter 6

Creative Chaos:
A Holy Mess

> Dance, when you're broken open.
> Dance, if you've torn the bandage off.
> Dance in the middle of the fighting.
> Dance in your blood.
> Dance, when you're perfectly free.
>
> — Jelalludin Rumi

Confusion is a way station in just about every creative process. In Greek mythology, the ancient god Chaos presided over the infinity of formless confusion that spawned the beginning of the universe. Chaos gave birth to Night and Death, and from their union Love, Order, and Beauty were born. Eventually, Love created Light and Day. What a beautiful metaphor for the creative process!

At some point in the journey, we inevitably find ourselves in the primal, formless chaos of uncertainty. This confusion might rear its head at the beginning, middle, or end of an endeavor. There are no formulas. As we grope around in the darkness seeking enlightenment, we often doubt ourselves. The 16th century mystic St. John of the Cross eloquently

TWILIGHT DANCE

described the "dark night of the soul" as a stage on the mystical path when earnest seekers feel lost in formidable trials and fear that God has abandoned them. This spiritual crisis heralds an impending breakthrough and awakening; the light of day is always born from the darkness of night.

The creative process sometimes brings us to a *creative* dark night of the soul where we feel lost in the chaos of our journey and abandoned by our original inspiration. We're looking for meaning, purpose, or direction, questioning everything and searching for a good reason to continue. We think about throwing the whole project out the window when our sunny beginning has mysteriously deposited us in a medieval dungeon. At those times, it's heartening to remember that out of the night's void, a renewed purpose and clarity will eventually emerge. I've found that these powerful periods always bring me back to the essence of what I'm trying to express.

Sometimes our creative passion stirs up old negative beliefs and becomes blocked by self-doubt or fear. Mystics have long understood this stage as the death of the ego or false self. We come up against the insecurities, negative beliefs, and internalized lies that prevent us from feeling confident and capable. We confront our shadow. Before we can move forward, we need to identify and work with these thought patterns.

Creative Crisis

The crisis of the creative dark night of the soul seems to be an inevitable rite of passage in the process of creation. This crisis is usually the central struggle when you hit that wall in the psychological stages of your creative process. It might feel like a breakdown of self-confidence or a shattering of your early vision as you find yourself doubting everything you've done so far. Uncomfortable uncertainty arises, and you might distrust your own impulses and begin to lose faith in your process. Your crisis may take the form of feeling pessimistic, directionless, purposeless, or hopeless. It often feels like a little death. You might want to give up. You're experiencing a *creative crisis.*

You might be wrestling with nagging inner voices that are saying: *I can't. I won't. I shouldn't. I'm a sham—wait till they all find out. I'm not doing anything original. Everyone else is better. I want to destroy everything I've done so far.* Suddenly your paintings look terrible. You can't believe you thought they were pretty good yesterday. Your knitted sweater looks pathetic and weird. Your poem seems like drivel. Your photographs are horrifyingly boring and disappointing. Everyone who told you that they liked them must have been lying.

If you find yourself thinking that you're an untalented impostor who should go hide on a deserted island, there's a good chance that you're moving through the dark night of a creative crisis. Take a deep breath, walk outside, look up at the sky, or gaze into the eyes of someone who loves you, and find solace in the wisdom that you're moving through a *universal stage* in your creative process. Remember: This, too, shall pass.

It's also reassuring to remind yourself that when you're confronting a creative dark night of the soul, it usually means that you're approaching the threshold of a deep truth or revelation. These are growing pains. You're shaking up the status quo of your beliefs and perceptions. Your crisis is a valuable portal into new insights and self-growth, and your discomfort may be heralding a powerful breakthrough. Chaos might be the symptom of these coming changes.

I've found that having meaningful *touchstones* is extremely helpful during the turbulent times of a creative crisis. Your touchstone reminds you of the light of your being and the deepest qualities of your soul. It might be a special place in nature, an inspiring book, a beautiful work of art, or a seashell you found on the beach. The poetry of the Persian mystic Rumi is a reliable and indispensable touchstone for me. Friendships and community are also vital when you're grappling with this stage. Sometimes good friends can be each other's touchstones.

The experience of navigating through a creative crisis can certainly be a struggle, but it has the potential to yield profoundly positive results. It's important to ask yourself to look behind the surface of your sudden crisis of faith by asking: *What's really happening? What's churning in the dark night of my self-doubt?* Usually, you'll discover that you're confronting potent false messages stored deep inside your unconscious.

Our old, disabling beliefs are the waste products of former wounds and shames. These troubling thoughts and feelings tend to arise because the act of creativity directly challenges our hidden patterns of self-negation or self-sabotage. Creation and destruction coexist naturally at every level of our universe. Pablo Picasso understood this profound truth when he reportedly said, "Every act of creation is first of all an act of destruction." When we open to our creative self, we're inviting the release of its opposite—destructive, unconscious beliefs about who we are that block our perception of our true potential.

The creative process often involves a dance with your shadow self. Although you may be tempted to resist this tango, try engaging instead. You'll notice that you become stronger and more resilient when you dare to face your shadow dragons. The more you know about your inner demons, the less power they have over you. The universal principle of destruction can actually be a positive and important impulse. For example, some forest fires are necessary to maintain the health of the forest. What old beliefs do you need to burn away in order to improve your creative ecology? What false self-images do you wish to destroy? Creation invokes destruction, and destruction invokes more creation. Remember, you're on a mission to uncover your true essence.

Creative dark nights of the soul may be excruciatingly painful times when we feel lost, raw, and despondent, but they can also be opportunities to fortify our inner core. Usually, these crises indicate that we're ready for the next level of growth. In my experience, I find that our psyches rarely take on more than we can handle, and we have a great capacity to move through such places. Often we're encountering a perfectly choreographed (though maddening!) test that will challenge us to grow or develop the qualities we most need.

Even though it feels difficult, keep reminding yourself that you're strong, resilient, and awake to whatever lesson this experience is teaching. When you're dealing with a creative crisis, ask yourself what important truths are clamoring to be faced. Are you being challenged to bring forth parts of yourself that are latent or unexpressed? For example, a shy person may find a new voice when confronted with an urgent need to be seen and heard.

Recently, I was coaching a man who'd been a successful actor for 30 years. He was filled with anxiety as he confronted a profound creative dark night of the soul. For the first time in his career, Andrew was having trouble finding work as an actor. He sensed that he needed to transition into a new career, but he was terrified. During one of our sessions, we sat looking out the window at the passing traffic as we dialogued, and Andrew remarked that it seemed as if everything was rushing ahead without him. He whispered to me that he had a secret feeling that his creativity was dead. I urged him to explore this creative death through writing and sculpting, two loves that he hadn't touched for many years.

The following week he arrived with a cardboard box. I will never forget what he pulled out to show me. He had sculpted a riveting image of a man yanking his own skeleton from his body. We spoke for several hours about the intense process that led up to the creation of this exquisitely honest piece, and he started to come back to life as he spoke. He reconnected with his creative passion. Eventually, he began writing a screenplay about a courageous cancer survivor who befriends a refugee from the Holocaust. Andrew's willingness to create from the bowels of his crisis inspires me to this day.

If you're passing through a creative dark night of the soul, my best advice is to let it carry you deep inside the illuminated center of truth's flame, where you'll find great wisdom and strength. Your creative crisis may actually be a blessing in disguise as it catalyzes you to excavate dynamic images that you might not have seen otherwise. Let go of your judgments, concepts, expectations, and assumptions, and bring the personal material you uncover into your creative process. Explore and develop the themes of your raw honesty in your writing, painting, music, screenplay, wood carving, or stand-up comedy routine. Strip away the chatter of your self-sabotaging beliefs and release your truth. Don't worry about editing or refining your explorations—you'll have plenty of time to do that later. Take risks and be bold. As Rumi said: "Enough of phrases and conceits and metaphors, I want burning, burning, burning."

Lost in a Familiar Unknown

Your response to being lost is a measure of your relationship to the unknown. Creativity cultivates your capacity to thrive in times of uncertainty. Since one of the requirements of the creative process is a willingness to open yourself to the unknown, is it any wonder that you might occasionally feel lost as you grope around in the landscape of your imagination? Sometimes creativity is a blind search, so welcome the condition of disorientation as you throw off the shackles of your preconceived conclusions and assumptions. Your state of bewilderment may hold an important message or lesson for your next steps.

Many useful insights can be gained by *practicing getting lost on purpose.* Have you ever been lost in the woods? If you have, you might remember that apart from feeling frightened, you probably felt very alive, awake, and alert. Being lost forces you to come into the present moment.

Many years ago I had an unforgettable experience in the woods of Poland when I worked with the great theater director Jerzy Grotowski in his Theater of Sources Project. (You may have seen the cult-film classic *My Dinner with Andre,* which featured conversations about Grotowski's extraordinary work.) I joined a large group of actors and artists who'd been invited from every continent. We didn't have a common language, but we did share a common goal: to investigate collective creative experiences together and discover what Grotowski called "the source of technique and the technique of source."

Our first experiment involved each of us being brought blindfolded by guides into the depths of the woods where we were left alone to explore our spontaneous instincts, the nature of our minds, and our relationship to the unknown. We

OTHER WORLD

had a nonverbal understanding that our allies were nearby at all times, but we couldn't hear or see them, and we weren't told when they'd return. We were asked not to speak.

At first I was uneasy, and my mind was filled with a crowd of thoughts: *What am I doing wandering around with an old rag wrapped around my eyes in a forest in Poland?* All of my senses became acutely aware. Every sound, vibration, and feeling was amplified as I made my way blindfolded through the dark night of my unfamiliar surroundings. Although I was unable to see, my inner visual sense was activated as my imagination projected a cavalcade of images on the movie screen of my mind. In the absence of my outer sight, I was eventually guided by my *in*sight. My hands reached out to feel what was around me: *Ah, yes . . . this is a tree branch. These are fresh leaves. Here's an old rock—it feels like granite. I just stepped on some twigs. The soil smells moist. . . .* My fingertips became my eyes, and my skin became my trusted translator.

While I was unacquainted with these particular Polish woods, I had many years of experience hiking in forests, and I drew upon this confidence. I learned a tremendous amount about my creative process and myself in those several hours. I discovered that if my sixth sense tells me I'm safe, I have access to a calm, deliberate state of inner resourcefulness when I'm lost. And in spite of my uncertainty, I did feel safe that night. As I slowed down and paid attention to everything, I noticed that I was directed by my curiosity and a steady stream of creative impulses. My disorientation became an adventure, and I began to enjoy myself and have fun. My sense of humor soon emerged and became my companion as I walked, danced, and explored. I realized that getting lost could be a rich and meaningful lesson that offers a powerful mirror for my inner process.

The experience of being lost plunges you instantly into *beginner's mind* where you experience everything as if for the first time. Shunryu Suzuki, the wonderful Zen roshi (teacher) said, "In the beginner's mind there are many possibilities, but in the expert's there are few." You come to each moment with fresh awareness and an eagerness to learn. Beginner's mind gives you the opportunity to see and hear with new eyes and ears as you move beyond your habitual reactions and thoughts. The next time you encounter confusion or feel lost in your creative process, call forth your beginner's mind.

Navigating the Mess

The creative process is messy—there's nothing neat or tidy about it. It's imperfect and unpredictable because we're human. You might be thinking, *But I keep my crafts area very organized.* Let me clarify right away that the messiness I'm talking about is within our *inner* process—it's not a measure of our cleanliness virtue.

So what's in this mess? The creative journey is filled with the usual rubble and debris that accumulate at building-construction sites. Piles of false starts, great ideas, amended plans, lost focus, unfinished schemes, and revised expectations collect on the sidelines as you labor over your project. Mounds of tough choices, unsolved problems, and strenuous decisions rise up behind you as you resolve to keep moving forward. An obstacle course of sticky self-confidence spills and jagged frustration shards ominously challenges your sure-footedness, and puddles of disappointment might occasionally splash onto your freshly pressed intentions.

Then there are the poker-hot steel beams of resistance and rejection that jab you continually with taunts of "No! No! No!

Wrong! Wrong! Wrong!" But if you look closely underneath the litter of your inner process, you'll find an indestructible container that holds your truth, enthusiasm, optimism, and tenacity. As long as passion is the foreman at your creative-construction site, you'll always know how to find this essential container.

Inspiration rarely arrives in a neat, orderly package that says, "Heat for five minutes and serve." The key to gaining mastery of your creative process is to find a reliable method that helps you plot a course through this marvelous mess of euphoria, despair, frustration, and exhilaration. Expect everything and nothing. The best way to navigate through the inevitable mess of creativity is to keep your eyes, ears, body, mind, and heart open.

The Girl Scout motto is: "Be prepared," but the creative process is a dance with the unknown. How can you prepare for the unexpected? Just as Girl Scouts might carry a flashlight, rope, water, rain gear, matches, and a first-aid kit when they go camping in the woods, artists must remember to bring beginner's mind, touchstones, and an awareness of the psychological stages of the creative process. The artist's preparation is mastering the ability *to be fully present in the moment.* You need to deal with whatever happens and move on. Everything is fodder for the creative process. When you look around and it appears that your creative process is in shambles, don't despair. You're not alone; you're part of a long tradition of creative souls who toil in the muddle of making something that won't be made easily.

Sometimes the inner mess spills out and does become an outer one. I notice that when I'm in the heat of creating a new theater performance, my office and rehearsal spaces become filled with papers, costumes, props, notebooks, and graphic designs. While everyone else might see my overflowing environment as a chamber of chaos, I always know exactly where everything is. In busy times, my inner organizer instinctively builds a dependable intuitive system that helps me navigate freely.

Because I'm juggling many deadlines and doing lots of multitasking, I must be able to see all the parts of my project simultaneously. For this reason, every available surface in my office becomes filled with the stuff of creation. If it's filed away out of sight, my experience has shown me that I'll surely forget about it. But as soon as my project is over, I immediately return to my usual preference for having a totally clear, uncluttered desk. My "all things on surfaces" method is no longer necessary. As you experiment with finding a useful system for your creative mess, remember: Sometimes it takes the chaos of a mess to find order and clarity.

Changing Patterns

Because periods of chaos are unavoidable, it's important to embark on your creative journey with a clear intention, specific goals, and organized work habits. These disciplines will help you steer your creative ship through rocky waters. However, expect your original vision to evolve as you proceed. The creative process isn't logical; there are no rules or formulas. While you'll probably encounter some universal experiences along the way, there's no fixed choreography for how these stages might play out. Your creative process is as unique as you are. The key is getting to know *your* particular tendencies. When you become more conscious about your process, you begin to recognize familiar emotional patterns and thoughts. This awareness equips you with insights that help you make proactive choices to sidestep predictable pitfalls.

Some people have a pattern of feeling hopelessly stuck just before they're about to have a major breakthrough, while some habitually feel dread and avoidance that makes the act of beginning difficult. Others chronically have trouble sustaining momentum or making a commitment. Another common pattern involves having periodic meltdowns that mask an unexpressed need for help or validation. I've worked with many people who have a habit of suppressing their rising creative joy and enthusiasm with a heavy dose of worry or fear. Many other creators repeatedly find themselves perilously perched at the stressful edge of last-minute deadlines. Learning to identify and change your counterproductive patterns is essential on the path of mastery. As Aristotle said, "We are what we repeatedly do. Excellence then is not an act, but a habit."

When you're involved in your creative process, what are *your* familiar patterns? At what point along the way does your self-confidence or motivation tend to get shaky? Does your psyche follow an unconscious blueprint of emotional states during your creative adventures? Is there a hidden method to your seeming madness? Do you recognize repetitive moods, thoughts, fears, or pitfalls? What are your patterns around beginning and ending? By learning how your individual process usually unfolds, you may find that you get less distracted or derailed by the parade of emotional states and mental attitudes that take up residence in your creative self.

As you reflect upon your past creative projects, you might find it helpful to write about your experience. Notice any patterns or recurring themes. It's important to do this without judging yourself. Becoming conscious of your default reactions and thought patterns gives you a tremendous advantage, so simply observe and write down some of your recognizable emotional or behavioral landmarks. Think of this exercise as creating a map that will give you much needed perspective the next time you find yourself hampered by confusion or chaos. Use your awareness of these guideposts to help you move through the process.

I know a woman who chronically loses her car keys and eyeglasses during stuck periods in her creative process. I suggested that she examine whether she unconsciously needs to search repeatedly for a key to unlock the stuck place in her project. When she spoke about her inability to see without her missing glasses, we laughed about the possibility that she might benefit from viewing her painting from a different perspective.

What are your typical triggers and struggles? Do your knee-jerk responses and attitudes help or hinder you? Do you see a need for some changes? Identify what strategies will facilitate overcoming chronic roadblocks. What will help you change your patterns? Keep a journal about your experiences, goals, and progress. Most important, give yourself some slack as you try to learn new creative work habits.

Once you've identified your unconscious patterns, it's important to replace them with strategies for navigating the challenging twists and turns of your creative process. For example, if you have chronic self-defeating thoughts, experiment with saying positive affirmations. An affirmation is an empowering statement of intention that you think or voice aloud. Best-selling author Louise Hay has done groundbreaking work in the use of affirmations. In her book, *I Can Do It*, she says, "An affirmation opens the door. It's a beginning point on the path to change." For feelings of inadequacy, she suggests affirming: *"I am in the process of positive change, and I deserve the best."* Find the affirmations that help you dismantle your unwanted patterns.

If the blank page presents a seemingly insurmountable hurdle to overcome, practice jumping in spontaneously. If you have a hard time beginning, pretend that you're already in the middle and just keep going. In the improvisation of life, we're always in the middle: Something has happened before, and something else will happen next. Try lighting a candle to establish a clear starting point for your activity. Sometimes a reticence about beginning veils a secret compulsion to do everything perfectly. Don't be afraid to fill your first creative canvases with the unbridled scribbles of mediocrity. Your first impulses don't have to be profound.

If you notice that you often have a slump cycle in the middle of your project, look for ways to anticipate that challenge by energizing yourself. Sometimes it helps to give yourself permission to put away your current project for a short period of time while you switch over to an enjoyable or non-goal-oriented activity. You might benefit from some cross-fertilizing.

I know an author who goes into the woods behind her home to belt out songs from Broadway musicals whenever she starts to feel lost or unproductive in her writing. She tells me that this trick never fails to jump-start her creative engines. It took her many years to realize that she had a pattern of feeling dried-up and uninspired as soon as she arrived at the midpoint of her book or article. Boldly singing aloud helps her scale the walls of inertia by energizing her passion and stimulating her creative inspiration—and it also reminds her to have fun and not take herself too seriously.

IMPERMANENCE

chapter 7

"And Now a Word from the Inner Critic . . ."

*"Creative minds have always been known
to survive any kind of bad training."*

— Anna Freud

Whenever I speak to audiences or workshop participants about the creative process, I usually ask how many people have an *inner critic.* Invariably, the room becomes filled with a sea of hands shooting up as people nod and sigh in a chorus of "Uh-huh" and "Oh, yeah." It seems that the inner critic is a well-known celebrity among creativity seekers.

I often do an improvisation exercise in my workshops: We roll out the red carpet and let all the inner critics arrive in their flashy limousines. We imagine them pompously strutting down the aisle as we all stand on the sidelines in deference to their great powers. It usually doesn't take long before someone in the class ignites an insurrection, and everyone joins in the satisfying act of evicting the inner critics from the room. Hoots, hollers, and rousing cheers of defiant victory energize the space. We've cleared the way for the magic of the creative spirit.

Let's talk about this familiar nuisance on the path of creativity. The inner critic's main mission is to convince you that whatever you do isn't good enough, so you might as well give up. It instigates a creative crisis, trying to thwart your journey and spoil the fun. I've found that most people have a vibrant and persuasive inner critic who wants to get into the act. Your professional achievements, social status, emotional awareness, age, or creative experience don't matter when it comes to these ravaging negative thoughts that attack your confidence. Sir Laurence Olivier, one of the greatest actors of all time, suffered from periods of severe stage fright. Such bouts of anxiety are often the crafty handiwork of the inner critic.

Most of us are all too familiar with this unwanted guest who loves to crash the party and deflate our balloons. The inner critic is the internal voice or body sensation that tells you that you're a useless, stupid, untalented loser who deserves to be laughed out of the room if you dare to express yourself or do anything inventive. It poses as a full-time, live-in reviewer who relentlessly monitors, judges, and pans your every creative impulse. Before your nascent idea has a chance to spring out of your imagination, there's already a front-page headline in your *New York Inner Times* that reads "Total Failure."

Vexing Visits and Uncanny Timing

The inner critic might show up before, during, or after our acts of creative expression. Some people have an inner-critic spell that hinders them at the beginning of a project. They feel thwarted by a crisis of self-confidence even before they can get out of the starting gate. As they contemplate taking a risk to be creative, learning a new skill, or going public with their talents, they might hear the inner critic saying: *Who are you kidding? You can't do that! You'll fall on your face, so don't even try.*

Others find that the inner critic usually makes its appearance while they're in the midst of creating or expressing themselves. While they're learning new dance steps or applying paint to the canvas, their internal recording plays that same old loop again: *Ugh! This is pure crap! Stop immediately. You have two left feet. You have no color sense. This is hopeless. Go wash the dishes—at least you can do that!* Instead of being in the moment, they're looking for the dial to switch off the inner critic's wearisome lecture.

Many people find that the inner critic remains relatively silent during the creative event, but drops in like clockwork after everything is finished. I've noticed that many performing artists and professional speakers deal with postpartum pessimism. Even if the audience was cheering in a standing ovation, an inner-critic commando in combat boots faithfully parachutes into the afterglow with the bad news: *Why are you celebrating? Didn't you know? You were terrible! Remember that sentence you flubbed in the first act? Didn't you see the man in the front row yawning? And your attempts at boldness embarrassed the woman on the aisle. Didn't you see that she was frowning? You need to leave this gathering immediately and stay awake all night feeling shame and regret.*

Have you ever experienced sweaty palms, a dry mouth, a racing heart, and a blank mind when someone asks you make an impromptu toast at a wedding or sing in front of an audience? These physical sensations are somatic responses to deep-seated inner critic beliefs. The inner critic might be saying: *Keep your mouth shut, be quiet, and let others take the focus. You're not good with words, and you don't know what you're talking about anyway. And sing? You must be out of your mind! Remember that second grade teacher who told you to mouth the words silently? She was right—don't make a peep.*

These debilitating messages may be lurking quietly in your unconscious. Or you might be all too aware of them blaring loudly in your brain. Before you can think, your mouth suddenly feels parched and your mind becomes a barren, arid place. Presto! If you dare to utter a sound, the inner critic will cleverly ensure a tongue-tied result.

Surprisingly, sometimes the inner critic becomes most rambunctious when we're successful. I've found that the volume and force of the critic's jabbering is unrelated to how well we do or how much positive feedback we receive. I've witnessed countless students in my improvisational acting classes struggle with accolades after a brilliant performance because their inner critic had already sniped them. The outer achievement triggered a barrage of self-condemning thoughts, guilt, shame, or uneasiness. Although they were shining in their acting scene, they still felt unsatisfied with their work. Their inner critic had dutifully found a way to steal their sense of accomplishment.

Each of us has a favorite list of negative adjectives that our inner critic employs. These criticisms usually happen to echo whatever disparaging remarks we heard as children growing up at home or in school—what a surprise. Now that we're older, we no longer need the original critics. We've managed to incorporate the self-deprecating messages into our own psyche with perfect precision. We can't gain mastery in the creative process (or in our lives, for that matter) without dealing effectively with the inner critic.

Our first instincts when confronting this part of our nature are often counterproductive. Here are a few understandable—but futile—knee-jerk reactions that may occur when we're faced with this renegade reviewer:

- Trying to ignore it, hoping it will just go away
- Trying to destroy it or out-bully it
- Medicating it with substances, overworking, or other distractions
- Using it to lash out at other people
- Deciding that it's correct: We *are* worthless, uncreative slobs

There's a wonderful Rwandan proverb that applies to our work with the inner critic: "You can out-distance that which is running after you, but not what is running inside you." You can't run away from the inner critic—it persists until you find a successful way to manage it. I've found that you need to shift your perspective radically when dealing with this troublemaker. What if you considered that *the inner critic is actually a powerful source of energy within you?* And what if you could harness this enormous energy on your own behalf? I like to call this method "emotional aikido," where you join with the energy behind the thought instead of resisting it.

Reptiles in Our Brains

I worked with a coaching client who suffered from a debilitating inner critic who ranted inside his head, telling him that he was a terrible writer who'd never succeed. Larry described horrible episodes of self-loathing when he'd be gripped by a belief that his work was "incoherent blabbering." When I asked him to visualize it, he had a vivid image of his inner critic: He saw a towering, scowling schoolmarm standing over him with a punishing iron ruler, and at each inch marker on the ruler, rusty nails with sharp points ominously protruded. He imagined that every time he wrote a sentence, she'd swat him on the hands and yell, "You just wrote garbage!" With each whack, a piece of her decrepit reptilian skin would flake off onto poor cringing Larry. I was impressed by his sharp creative imagination as he described his inner critic with precise details.

During our sessions, I invited Larry to embody the intense energy of this scaly schoolmarm by expressing it through movement and sound. This was challenging for him since these bouts of self-condemnation zapped his energy and left him feeling listless. He felt weighed down by exhaustion even though he was getting plenty of sleep, but I encouraged him to tap in to the considerable energy that was tied up in the schoolmarm's critical messages. Gradually, he began to move, vocalize, run around the studio, invent spontaneous verbal rants, and do whatever was necessary to release the toxic energy of his inner critic.

Next, I asked him to act out the schoolmarm character. His eyes lit up at the invitation, a mischievous look came over his face, and he instantly transformed himself into a hilarious, dead-on parody of his inner critic. He twisted his mouth and nose into a lizardlike scowl, and in a nasal voice, railed on about "Larry's incoherent style," his "stupidity," and the ridicule that he'd surely receive if he tried to publish his work. Then he switched roles and spoke back to his inner critic with passion and defiance.

As we debriefed the exploration, Larry realized that the schoolmarm was a deft composite of his hypercritical father and his "never satisfied" college English composition teacher, Mrs. Lacey. He noticed that most of his inner critic's accusations were remarkably similar to the cutting comments he relentlessly heard from his father, as well as the critical red markings Mrs. Lacey scratched in the margins of his essays.

Larry said he felt "highly energized" after our work and motivated to write—and he noticed that the volume of his inner critic's voice was lowered to an imperceptible squeak. He went home and did lots of writing that week. Most important, he felt great about what he read on the pages. During our ongoing sessions together, Larry learned to harness the power of his inner critic and use it constructively.

Once in a while, there *is* a kernel of accuracy in the inner critic's distorted harangue. Your job is to discard the false beliefs and exaggerated lies about your overall worth as you look for any morsels of truth that might be helpful to your process. For example, Larry's schoolmarm critic used to tell him he was a lazy, untalented embarrassment to his literary family; she also chided him for writing incoherent rambling babble. We decided to unpack these criticisms, one stinky lie at a time.

Larry and I agreed there was no truth to the attack on his ability. He's a wonderful writer with a keen ability to create characters, and deep down inside, he knew he had talent. The accusation of laziness was absurd since he worked diligently every day. If anything, he needed to learn to take more time off from writing so that he could enjoy his social life.

However, there *was* some truth to the nagging sensation that he was an embarrassment to his family. When I asked Larry to delve into that feeling, it soon became clear that his fear of humiliating them as a writer wasn't the real issue. A more painful subject loomed within him: His family was unaware that he was gay; he hid it from them because he believed that his parents would react negatively. When I asked him what he thought their biggest concern would be, he immediately responded, "They'll be embarrassed to tell their friends; they'll think it reflects badly on the family."

Larry was transferring his pain about his family's disapproval of his lifestyle onto his writing. His inner critic became the repository for his fear, hurt, shame, anger, and self-hatred. He realized that he had to come out to his parents if he hoped to overcome his self-doubts as a writer. He was startled to discover that his self-critical feelings about being an embarrassment were directly affecting his creative imagination by causing him to censor his ideas and character choices. In this case, his inner critic was serving a hidden purpose by catalyzing him to deal with important personal-growth needs. He decided to face his parents.

The final criticism from his schoolmarm indicted him for "writing incoherent rambling babble." Larry had to admit that the "incoherent" condemnation was silly considering all the positive feedback he'd gotten from people in writing groups over the years who understood and appreciated his work. But I observed that Larry also had a tendency to go off on long-winded tangents when he spoke. When I read some of his fiction writing, I saw that although he was a gifted writer with a stunning imagination, he had an inclination to ramble at times, instead of getting to the point. This occasional habit distracted the reader from the beauty and forward momentum of his passages.

When I shared my observation with him, he knew exactly what I was talking about. After exploring what he called his "rambling routine," he realized that it was probably an unconscious attempt to send readers off on a "dusty, dead-end road" so they wouldn't arrive at the "mansion" of his true talent. He laughed and said, "That way, I can avoid the scary possibility that I might be as good a writer as my dad—or God forbid, even better!"

Rely on Your Inner Ally

Larry and I tried an experiment: Each time he began to go off on a tangent, he would write or say aloud: *I am a gifted writer who deserves to be understood and appreciated by others.* This technique invokes the help of your *inner ally* who affirms your true gifts. As you work with the inner critic, it's vital to empower your inner ally with clear, regular affirmations about your creativity. This supporter cheers you on, lifts you up, and pats you on the back for your earnest efforts. Many people have an overdeveloped inner critic and an underdeveloped inner ally, so look for ways to strengthen your inner ally by giving it opportunities to exercise its influence in your life.

As Larry learned to incorporate his inner ally into his writing process, he began to notice that he drifted into unnecessary tangents less frequently as he wrote. His dedication to unscrambling the hidden negative beliefs embedded in the messages from his inner critic brought him invaluable insights about the lies and truths he needed to face clearly. The more he stood in his truth with his inner ally by his side, the less he meandered in his work. He also found that his self-esteem improved, and he began to like himself more. When he told me about these new feelings, I was reminded of Oscar Wilde's famous witticism: "To love oneself is the beginning of a life-long romance."

Remember the amazing details and hilarious image that Larry concocted when he imagined the character of his reptilian schoolmarm? Well, he named her Hilda, and she eventually ended up in one of his short stories. Here's a stunning news flash: *Your inner critic is an extremely creative part of you.* Think about its remarkable ability to invent countless ways to zap you. No matter how much therapy or self-awareness work you do, the inner critic is a genius at finding new methods for placing land mines of self-doubt or fear in your path. In fact, it's a brilliant master improviser who possesses a lightning-quick ability to derail you. It enters boldly into the scenes of your mind with tenacious commitment as it attempts to dismantle your self-assurance. Your inner critic is clever, flexible, creative, resilient, and crafty as it switches from one tactic to another in its mission of destruction. But why wouldn't it be creative in all these ways? It's part of you! Imagine how much vitality you might gain if you could release your creativity from its grasp.

Try noticing the creativity of your inner critic the next time it sneaks up on you. How does it undermine you? Does that harsh voice tend to arise before, during, or after your creative projects? When you study its tactics and messages, do you recognize the origin of these critical thoughts? Do you have reliable inner (and outer) allies to help you defuse the critic's bombs?

If your inner critic seems like a formidable character, try disarming it with a detailed parody. Imagine it as the villain in an action movie. Most of these films have a predictable plot: An underappreciated evil genius living in a cave beneath the earth at the South Pole is scheming to blow up the city where the unsuspecting hero lives. Look at your inner critic as a desperado who's trying to wreak havoc in your creative life. What's the symbolic plot in this familiar story? What methods does your adversary employ? Do you have secret rendezvous meetings with your tempestuous rogue?

Invent a creative-ally superhero who stands up to the critic and identify your supporter's effective strategies. Which affirmations will enable your ally to disable your critic's weaponry? Imagine a scene where you and your ally prevail over this treacherous saboteur in a dramatic climax of truth, honor, and creativity. Write, paint, dance, sculpt, sing, draw, or enact it—and be specific. Design a small superhero cape for your creative ally, or create a song about your emotional aikido with these characters. The key is to unleash and harness the creativity of the inner critic.

TENACITY

chapter 8

Befriending Your
Inner Editor

*"Creativity is allowing yourself to make mistakes.
Art is knowing which ones to keep."*

— Scott Adams

The inner critic cannot operate without our collaboration. As strange as it may sound, we often harbor an *unconscious loyalty* toward this character. Even after years of therapy, we may continue to sort and scan for negative messages. *The inner critic is like a secret lover* with whom we have a love-hate toxic relationship: We know that we should break up, but we keep going back for more.

Have you ever had an experience where you obsessively focused on one small critical comment, even though a roomful of people praised your achievement? You heard wonderful appreciation for your work, but all you could think about was that tiny criticism that rapidly turned into a major wrecking ball in your mind. Or maybe there were times when you initially felt great about something you created until you noticed a nagging thought that there *must* be something wrong with it.

Sometimes when we excel, we wait for the other shoe to drop. Why do we do this? What compels us to scan for what's wrong, rather than celebrate what's terrific? What makes us search breathlessly for one more tantalizing tryst with this critical inner voice? The inner critic's siren call is seductive since it releases us from the responsibility of fulfilling our dreams and life purpose. By confirming our secret suspicion that we're not good enough, it gives us an excuse to avoid putting ourselves out there. While we may think that we're afraid of failing, our bigger fear may be the possibility of success.

The inner critic echoes a familiar tirade that we heard from someone who played a key role in our upbringing. Succumbing to this lure is an unconscious way of staying loyal and obedient to judgmental authority figures, such as parents, teachers, or others who may have been unable to translate their love into supportive messages. Most likely, their early lives were shaped by the weight of similar criticisms. I often tell my students to beware of unconscious loyalties to people in our lives who may have unwittingly contributed to keeping us small, weak, unhappy, or unsuccessful.

Many common expressions reveal this insidious message: "You're getting too big for your britches." "Don't get a swelled head." "Who do you think *you* are?" Sound familiar? As you learn to master the art of dancing with your inner critic, your job is to sort out the love from the lies about your creative abilities and potential.

As you become clear about the specifics of your inner critic's lies and toxic messages, you'll eventually be ready to end this stormy relationship. Now you can give more attention to your *inner editor.* This character helps you make clear, intelligent choices by offering *constructive* suggestions; it shapes and refines your creative ideas. While the inner critic might try to convince you that none of your thoughts are worthwhile, your inner editor hunts for the impulses that would best convey your vision. The ability to make incisive choices is crucial in the creative process, so don't be afraid to edit your work. There's a well-known saying in the film industry that the measure of a great movie is how many terrific scenes ended up on the cutting-room floor.

Editing yourself and succumbing to your inner critic are two different things, but sometimes you might confuse them. The inner critic says that there's something innately wrong with who you are as a person, whereas the inner editor is a champion of your talents and wants you to succeed by producing your best work. The inner editor's job is to help improve and polish your creative endeavors by helping you make choices about what to develop, revise, reconsider, embellish, or delete. It's a discerning internal "eye" that gives you a keen decision-making instinct without self-judgment.

Unlike the inner critic, the inner editor is a *supportive* member of your creative team. Once you unmask your critic's beguiling machinations, you'll be able to recognize your editor's advice. You'll find that this ongoing learning process is an extraordinary laboratory for personal growth and change. You may even find yourself amused by the relentless tricks of the inner critic as you sidestep its booby traps.

Have you met your inner editor? Can you identify its suggestions amidst the chatter of the inner critic? Do you have a solid working relationship—are you open to suggestions? Write about your experiences with constructive self-editing, and tell a friend about how you distinguish your inner editor from your inner critic. I find that the capacity to distill and refine creative impulses depends heavily on the contribution of the inner editor. In addition, a healthy, active relationship with this part of yourself might help you receive and integrate suggestions from real-life editors, teachers, and directors.

PERSPECTIVE

chapter 9

Spider Wisdom: The Webs of Perfectionism and Comparison

"Jealousy is all the fun you think they had."
— Erica Jong

In Greek mythology, the spider represents creativity. A fascinating story recounts how this happened. The goddess Athena was a prolific weaver, and she challenged a talented young peasant named Arachne to a weaving contest. Athena heard that Arachne had dared to say that she achieved her skill through her own talent and hard work rather than through the tutelage of the goddess. She'd also asserted that she was as good a weaver as any immortal one. This angered Athena, who insisted that they have a public test of prowess.

When the garment from Arachne's loom equaled (or maybe even surpassed) the splendor of Athena's work, the goddess mercilessly beat the young woman with her weaving shuttle. Arachne was so devastated and shamed by this beating that she hanged herself in a fit of desperation.

The sight of Arachne's lifeless body hanging from a rope penetrated Athena's punitive heart, and the goddess felt saddened by the destructive nature of her jealousy. She decided to repent. She dislodged Arachne's body from the noose and covered it with a magic solution that instantly caused Arachne's nose and ears to fall off while her head shrank to a tiny size. She was reduced to a big belly with long, hairy legs that sprouted from her nimble fingers. Athena had transformed the dead weaver into a spider or *arachnid.* Arachne's superior weaving talents would live eternally in the lineage of all spiders.

It's interesting that Athena's generosity was not able to sufficiently overcome her competitive rage in order to restore Arachne back to her human life. Instead, the goddess chose to sacrifice the peasant woman while simultaneously paying homage to her creativity.

There are powerful lessons about creativity in this ancient tale. We're reminded that perfectionism is a futile pursuit of the impossible. It diverts us from a more important goal of excellence, which is an earnest striving for improvement. We also see that making comparisons with others can be deadly in the creative process. Creativity is strengthened by collaboration and weakened by envy.

Comparisons set up a contest where there must be a winner and a loser. One is better, and one isn't as good; one is more, and one is less. If we're preoccupied with feeling that our creative efforts aren't as good as the next person's, we're making ourselves the loser. But if we're wrapped up in thinking that we're better than someone else, we're making that person the loser. Either way, we're siphoning off precious energy and emotional resources. There are no losers in creativity—everyone is a winner.

While perfectionism, jealousy, conceit, insecurity, and competitiveness may be familiar obstacles, these adversaries fade into the background of your awareness when you focus on the simple acts of your task. The beauty and value of your creation doesn't depend on its comparison to another one.

The ultimate worth and importance of what you create begins with a meaningful intention and culminates in your sense of fulfillment.

Arachne didn't approach the contest with vanity; she came with love and passion for weaving. But Athena arrived with a burning need to put Arachne in her place by winning. The goddess was obsessed with making a *perfect* creation to prove her superiority, while Arachne wasn't concerned about perfection or even the outcome of the contest. She found herself in this predicament because she'd dared to feel confident and speak truthfully about her abilities. It was only when others attempted to evaluate whether Athena's weaving was inferior or superior that Arachne felt compelled to speak honestly about her own hard work and talent. Because she didn't choose to exhibit false modesty, she was thrust into an unwanted competition.

Arachne came to the competition event as she did every day to her loom—as a lover to her beloved. Unlike Athena, she was consumed with her devotion to weaving and the pure act of creation. Every moment spent guiding the shuttle through the warp and weft of the fabric was an act of lovemaking. Her craft was her friend; her mindfulness was free of the ego desires and distractions that cause suffering, disappointment, and negative comparisons.

In contrast, Athena wasn't focused on her own weaving, but rather on the progress and beauty coming forth from the other loom. I wonder if she was actually more jealous of Arachne's unwavering concentration and dedication. Whatever fueled her obsession, Athena diverted her attention away from the magnificence of her own garment as she fixated on Arachne's designs. Here we have the ageless lesson: When we focus on comparisons with others, we're fanning the fires of destruction. But when we create for the sake of creating—

without concern for the achievements of others—we're feeding the creation aspect of our being.

Athena and Arachne represent two facets of our inner life in the creative process. One part of us is like an untrained animal that runs here and there sniffing to see what everyone else is up to in case it's better than what we're doing. This part beats us up for not being good enough. The story also illustrates the deadly false belief that we shouldn't become "too successful," "too good," or "too big." Athena's reaction symbolizes the lie that we should stay small and never dare to fully own our talents. The Arachne side of our nature seeks to create for the satisfaction of creating. This true and centered part of us can sit for hours without being distracted by the achievements or comments of others.

How fitting that the industrious spider would come to symbolize creativity. They're relentlessly inventive as they spin their webs from silk made within their own bodies. These silk geometrical wonders have many functions, including catching prey and serving as draglines to lower themselves from the web. Sometimes the silk is used for parachuting or ballooning to help spiders fly through the air as they look for new food or transport their young.

Among the many intricate webs they spin are the orb, triangle, and sheet types. These remarkable adaptations beautifully epitomize the clever ingenuity of the creative mind. Undaunted by stumbling blocks, spiders fashion a solution out of the substance of their own bodies. What a powerful affirmation that everything we need for success is already within us.

Ironically, the most dangerous webs are *tangle* webs, which are home to the poisonous black widow spiders. As Wren mentions later in the book, some tangles can surely be precarious. Have you ever wondered why spiders don't get caught or stuck in the maze of their own spinning? This is because the middle spiral area of the web is sticky, but the outer spokes aren't. Very simply, the wise spider knows exactly where to step and what to avoid. It's also possible that the spider's tiny feet emit an oily substance, which helps them move around the gummy strands.

The creative adventurer must develop a similar dexterity. You need to know how to step around the traps of the inner critic and the pitfalls of self-doubt, and become sure-footed as you avoid the sticky web of comparisons with others. The wise creator knows how to find the center when the outer edges of an idea begin to fray. Trust is the substance that human creative "spiders" must generate in order to lubricate their travel through tight passages.

Do you see yourself in the tale of Arachne and Athena? Which character best reflects your current experience? Is there an Athena type who chronically enters your story as you create? Do feelings of jealousy, perfectionism, comparison, or competition play a role in your creative process? Do you sometimes feel like Athena as you compare yourself to someone else's achievements or recognition? What might happen if you gave up being perfect? Do the accomplishments of others sometimes distract or deflate you? What might happen if you practice bringing your focus and concentration into the sphere of *your own* creativity?

Do you ever feel like Arachne? Do you think that others might be jealous or threatened by the breadth of your talents? Have you turned any part of your talented self into a shrunken spider that hides in dark places when the spotlight of public attention shines in your direction? Have you internalized the messages that say you shouldn't become too successful, too good, or too big?

Draw upon your strengths, skills, and passion. Try saying aloud this affirmation: *"I am big, bold, and beautiful, and I take up as much space as I need for the fullness and truth of my creativity."* Make a clear, conscious decision to let your abilities shine. Remember that the lessons of spider wisdom are deep and powerful in the creative process. Your mission is to find access to the trust and agility you'll need to move industriously through your webs of creation.

WEB SIGHT

chapter 10

Resistance

> *"Art begins with resistance—at the point where resistance is overcome. No human masterpiece has ever been created without great labor."*
>
> — André Gide

E verybody has a *resistance shtick.* Your best friend, spouse, or creative collaborator will recognize it immediately. It might look like a rebellious child with heels dug in, saying, "You're not the boss of me!" It could be a grand opera of rationalizations, a proclamation of negative predictions, or a tap dance of denial. Perhaps it's a tragic soliloquy of insecurity: "I'd rather jump to my death than face the humiliation of certain failure." And sometimes resistance resembles a Mafia hit man threatening to "take care" of anyone who wants you to do that thing you don't want to do.

Why are we resistant? Do we have to keep performing the same old routines, like tired vaudeville stars with stale material and outdated costumes? How can we change our oppositional stances and melt our resistance?

Creativity is essentially a learning process: We learn by trial and error as we acquire new skills. Our creative act brings something into existence or makes something happen that wasn't there before we arrived. While learning something new, we often encounter frustration or resistance as we develop competency. Resistance is a common experience in the creative process—just about everybody passes into and out of this realm. While creativity thrives on a spirit of *yes,* resistance is powered by the energy of *no.* When we resist, we're saying *no* to whatever we're learning or creating. We're opposing instead of joining, blocking instead of building. Since creativity depends on free-flowing impulses, it's easy to see why this opposition can be problematic.

The degree and nature of our resistance depends on how we *originally learned to learn* as children. Our early conditioning around acquiring knowledge sets the stage for later patterns. If we were taught to accept our mistakes in a nonjudgmental, supportive atmosphere, we might tend to feel more patient and trusting as we try new skills. But if we heard lots of criticism, we might notice that we've internalized this condemnation by becoming especially hard on ourselves, or we might resist input or suggestions from others. If the accent was on results rather than process, we'll be driven by that lesson. Our resistance might show up as impatience or feeling pressured to produce. If our early learning environment was highly competitive or aggressive, we might be hyperfocused on everyone else's accomplishments instead of our own.

Some people learned to learn in highly stimulating classrooms or homes where questions, curiosity, and respect for creative thinking were clearly valued. Others plodded through uninspiring educational circumstances where the emphasis was placed on rote memorization and the regurgitation of meaningless facts. Whatever our conditioning, we can be sure that it helped shape our relationship to gaining new skills, using our imagination, and trusting our creative process.

However, we can consciously reprogram our creative hard drives by introducing new affirmations about our ability to learn. We can replace old, self-sabotaging habits with positive beliefs. I've seen countless people change their experience of learning and creativity in my many years of teaching and coaching. It requires a sincere resolve to bring greater awareness to counterproductive patterns and a willingness to change conditioned beliefs.

Before you can begin to work with your resistance, you need to identify exactly *what* you're resisting. On the surface it may seem as if you're resisting learning a new skill. Or you might think you're only opposing certain aspects of your creative project—for example, you like to write, but you hate thinking about grammar. Your resistance might show up as a feeling of irritation with someone who's trying to give you directions or assistance. But look further: Try to discover what *feeling, experience, or need* you're resisting.

Are you resisting criticism, fear, inadequacy, commitment, or sadness? Are you pushing away vulnerability, success, impatience, competition, anger, or disappointment? Look for a struggle against joy, confusion, satisfaction, or accepting help. What's your resistance teaching you? What important information or message is your psyche sending through this experience? What are you avoiding?

One thing's for sure: It's fruitless to resist your resistance. The challenge is to find a constructive way of working with it. Take a deep breath, soften your belly, and open yourself to the deeper truth that lives behind the resistance. Think of your resistance as a bandage that you grew over a wound to protect it from further injury. You probably learned to employ these emotional bandages to defend against hurt. As you heal and grow, you may not need that bandage anymore.

The Lessons of Yes and No

I once worked with a young man named Leo who would stiffen his spine, smirk, and roll his eyes every time I offered suggestions or directions for his acting scenes. I was perplexed by this habit since he was usually warm and open during our informal conversations. But in the context of practicing the skills of improvisation in front of an audience, his resistance was palpable. It permeated the workshop atmosphere, and I observed that the rest of the group became increasingly restrained in his presence. Creativity doesn't flourish in an atmosphere of criticism, blame, judgment, or resistance.

I invited Leo to examine his responses by asking him if he was aware of his resistance. He seemed genuinely surprised and said no, looking at me quizzically as I described my perceptions of his attitude and behavior. Then I asked him what he was feeling when I gave him directions. He quickly replied, "Nothing." Then he thought for a moment and added, "I'm not really feeling anything. I'm just dealing with a voice in my head that's screaming about how I don't know what I'm doing, and I'm messing up again."

I watched him try to blink away a hint of tears in his eyes as he glanced at his fellow classmates. Everyone was moved by his honest vulnerability, and one woman started to tell him how much she appreciated his courage to explore these feelings. Leo interrupted her, stiffened again, rolled his eyes, and blurted out, "I don't think I can do this improvisation thing. I'm too uptight. I think I'm dragging the class down."

When I gently pointed out that he'd just resisted a positive affirmation from a group member, Leo became pensive. I observed that his resistance seemed to arise when someone was offering support or help. He quietly nodded his head and agreed: "I never really had too much positive encouragement when I was growing up. I guess I'm always bracing for a criticism or a sniper attack." His eyes were tearful once more as he looked down at the floor.

I asked him if he'd like to take advantage of this remarkable moment to change some of his conditioned responses and beliefs about getting help. He hesitated for a moment, but decided to give it a try. I invited him to create a spontaneous monologue about believing he deserved to receive help and nonjudgmental support to learn new skills. At first he resisted my suggestion by saying he couldn't see the purpose of the exercise. He was sure it wouldn't be of any use—and then he said, "I can't do it." When I asked him to imagine that maybe he was really saying "I *won't* do it," he laughed in agreement.

It was clear to me that Leo simply needed to express *no* in a dozen different ways before he could say *yes.* Sometimes resistance is a reaction to feeling controlled. Privately, I wondered if he'd missed the early childhood developmental stage that includes learning to say no, since thwarting a child's need to learn about setting limits can result in an adult pattern of resistance or difficulty with personal boundaries.

I asked Leo to begin his stream of consciousness monologue by saying "I won't!" with force and gusto. He found his voice immediately. Then I asked him to continue by saying no to everything that came to his mind. This idea piqued his interest, and he proclaimed "No!" to getting up in front of the class members, "No!" to being watched, "No!" to listening to feedback, and "No!" to feeling pressured. His monologue flowed effortlessly and passionately. Next, I asked him to speak a litany of everyday things that bugged him. He railed against crazy drivers, prerecorded customer-service voice-mail systems, and the high price of professional sporting events. His resistant *no* stance was giving way to the energy of *yes* as he effortlessly created a spontaneous, entertaining monologue.

Next, I asked him to transition into the themes of getting help and support. He didn't skip a beat as he launched into this more vulnerable subject. His words carried strong feeling, conviction, and humor as he spoke about his right to get help. The class participants sat transfixed as he talked about his high school football coach who used to berate him whenever he made mistakes. He revealed a childhood struggle with undiagnosed dyslexia that left him feeling stupid, frustrated, and ashamed. He told us that he'd been drawn to improvisation to recover his spontaneity and overcome his fear of making a fool of himself. Gone were his smirks, rolling eyes, and stiff body. He was focused, articulate, and engaged with the audience as he moved freely around the space.

As he was finishing, I asked Leo to create a playful parody of his resistance shtick, and he launched into a hysterically funny and insightful enactment. I then invited everyone in the group to join him with their own resistance characters, and soon the room was buzzing with energy, sound, and motion. Leo had dared to find the enjoyment and freedom in saying *no*. By giving his resistant self a voice, he'd made it possible to say *yes* and speak from his heart. He was no longer controlled by his feelings of resistance; he was free to express his vulnerability, strength, and humor.

෴

Resistance is sometimes our psyche's way of expressing anger or frustration. We're insulted by the hurtful, demeaning messages of our inner critic. We feel inadequate to face the challenge. We feel controlled by deadlines or difficult collaborations. We're annoyed by our inability to grasp a new skill. We want to rebel. We say or think *I can't,* but unconsciously we're really feeling *I won't.*

I can't is something we say when we feel weak and incapable of meeting the moment with *I will.* But when we dare to identify with the strength of *I won't,* we have the opportunity to tap in to the power needed to overcome our resistance. If we admit that we won't do something, we have to ask *Why?*

When Leo owned the feeling of *I won't,* he released his resistance and opened the door to his truth. He realized that his struggles with dyslexia (as well his critical football coach) had contributed greatly to his insecurity. Resistance thrives in power struggles. When we give up that fight, we gain access to our unhampered creativity.

NARROW PASSAGE

chapter 11

The Ultimate Creativity Guru

*"If you want to make an apple pie from scratch,
you must first create the universe."*
— Carl Sagan

Sometimes your creative process might feel like a peaceful act of self-nurturance, a treasured retreat from the pressures and demands of everyday life. The quiet safety and sacredness of your creative practice is uplifting and comforting on those days. At other times, your creative process might resemble being inside a huge, churning blender: You feel stirred up, minced, and tossed around by the spontaneous combustion of your own imagination.

The changing complexion of the creative process mirrors the broader context of our earth and universe. For example, scientists have determined that when a human being is brainstorming, there are actually millions of tiny electrical neural events that resemble a lightning storm occurring in the brain. We're changing the "weather" in our brains each time we do some serious thinking to figure out a problem. Our brains reflect the activity of the larger universe. (This notion is depicted humorously and effectively in the film *What the Bleep Do We Know!?*)

The next time you feel like a bubbling cauldron of creative conflict, remember that the heat of the earth's inner core reaches nearly 5,000 degrees Celsius. The inner core is surrounded by molten iron and nickel. Scientists think that the inner core rotates faster than the surface of the earth, while the outer liquid core spins chaotically, but more slowly. The churning rotations of the earth's interior cause currents that make the tectonic plates move.

These dramatic geological activities provide an interesting metaphor for certain aspects of the creative process. There are times when you might have a hot core idea that's quickening within you, while other parts of your conceptual process are whirling erratically with impulses. During those moments, creativity feels like a roiling mix of inner struggle. Creativity often passes through periods of discord, and I think of this creative conflict as the friction that arises when different ideas or impulses rub against each other. This friction produces the heat (passion) and light (insight) of invention.

Earth is our home, and it's in an ongoing state of dramatic change, from its core to its surface. Massive floods, erupting volcanoes, fierce hurricanes, and rumbling earthquakes are unmistakable reminders of this truth. Other changes are happening at an almost imperceptible rate; it takes centuries for winds to carve a canyon out of rock formations, and millions of years to build mountains from tectonic forces. These slower transformations mirror another important lesson in the creative process: Sometimes there's a lot going on even when nothing seems to be happening. Progress may be taking place in spite of your perception that you're at a standstill.

When I look at my periodic creative fermentations in this grander context, I begin to experience a wave of relief. Our bodies are made from the material of the sun and earth—how could we expect to be less combustible than our awesome elemental parents? We need to make friends with our inner upheavals and intensities by first realizing the larger framework of universal change that supports our individual emotional and biochemical agitations. Otherwise, we're like tiny corks bobbing along on a great ocean, trying to understand the nature of our movements and responses without acknowledging the dynamics of the sea.

The creative process of the human being reflects the creation cycles of the cosmos. The stars, planets, moons, and other celestial bodies were born from a powerful and ongoing series of chemical experiments and elemental events. Themes of expansion and contraction are everywhere in the physical universe, and your creative process is part of those larger cosmic rhythms. On some days you might feel more expansive, hopeful, or productive; other days bring the opposite experience.

It's consoling to remember that your creativity is contained in a bigger universe of ongoing creative volatility. What you see in the night sky represents a relentless evolution of matter through stages of creation and destruction. The beauty of shooting stars, the revolving of our planet around the sun, the mysterious physics of light trapped inside black holes, the breathtaking spectacles of exploding stars (supernovas) all embody a tumultuous poetry of change. The cosmos is definitely the ultimate creativity guru!

You can learn a great deal about your own creative process by observing these cyclical stages of change in the universe. If you feel stuck, uninspired, or confused, just look up at the night sky. What you see will surely put everything you're feeling into context—a very *large* context. When you remind yourself that some of the light you're seeing could be coming from distant stars that no longer exist, you may be inspired to view the nature of time and reality with fresh eyes. Stars have a life cycle, and as they grow old and begin running out of hydrogen to burn, they expand. When they eventually run out of hydrogen and helium fuel, they collapse and explode. You might continue to see the light from "dead" stars because it takes many years for their light to reach your eyes.

This astronomical phenomenon is a beautiful metaphor for your creative process. Sometimes you give birth to a strong vision in the beginning stages of a project, and as time passes, your early conception often evolves into a completely different outcome. But notice how the light of your original inspiration may continue to show up and guide you long after you change direction.

In the late 1920s, Edwin Hubble discovered that the universe is *expanding* when he observed that distant galaxies are actually moving away from Earth. In fact, the farther away they are, the faster they're moving. This means that your individual explorations exist within a universe of perpetual expansion. You might want to remember that the next time your creativity dumps you at an apparent dead end.

This expansion theme seems to be mirrored in the human brain. For many years, the prevailing belief among neuroscientists was that animals and humans were born with a certain number of brain cells that would decrease with age, but never *increase.* Nobody imagined that brains could create new cells.

But when zoologist Fernando Nottebohm noticed that canaries seemed to learn new songs each season, he wanted to find out how. He eventually figured out that birds teach each other new songs. They even have the ability to remember the exact melody of a complex song, which is crucial to their mating ritual. After many experiments and studies, Nottebohm discovered that bird brains produce thousands of new brain

DEEP BREADTH

cells each day. This discovery led to a major breakthrough in the field of neuroscience as researchers began to realize that the human brain is also capable of creating new neurons through a process called neurogenesis. As our universe continues to expand, so do our brains. When we look at ourselves from this perspective, it seems that we're actually hardwired for learning, creativity, and growth.

The Fog of Creativity

Creativity is a process of intentional change. There are times when your attempts to be creative feel like a black hole where the gravity field is so dense and overwhelming that no light or good ideas can escape. On those days, you can't seem to find yourself, and your imagination might seem trapped or stuck. You're in the dark, uncertain about what to express next. Then, when you least expect it, a burst of insight appears like a cavalcade of shooting stars.

There are other times when you nurture a compelling new creative project until it becomes like a sun. You revolve around this radiant core idea until it matures into its final expression. Like an exploding star or supernova, your "Aha" moment may burst out of your imagination with brilliant clarity. Seeing yourself in the larger context of universal rhythms of expansion and contraction helps bring more self-acceptance, trust, and understanding to your creative endeavors.

The creative process can sometimes feel nebulous. As you struggle with a new idea or design, it's comforting to remember that the universe is filled with millions of nebulae. Each mass of stellar gas and dust goes through a long journey on its way to becoming a star or planet. There are days when you're bound to feel foggy, unclear, or unfocused. On the outside you may appear to be like a mini-nebula floating aimlessly in space, but try pausing to consider that on the inside there might be a deep and productive process of gestation going on. Your cloudy sensation may be a valuable cocoon that's enveloping you to protect your embryonic creative impulses and ideas.

A fascinating study conducted at Tufts University showed that memory and creative thinking are actually enhanced by periods of confusion or uncertainty. By using an EEG, researchers were able to identify the electrical pulse that accompanies a "Eureka!" experience. They also found that giving subjects confusing or misleading information actually strengthened their creativity as well as their ability to remember what they'd discovered.

A study participant was given baffling word riddles such as: "The girl spilled her popcorn because the lock broke." Later, a seemingly unrelated clue would be introduced: "lion cages." Suddenly the "Aha" moment burst forth as the person realized that the girl was at the zoo eating her popcorn near an escaping lion! Your brain's capacity for insight is fortified every time you wrestle with uncertainty and nebulous concepts. You also improve your memory of what you learn when your mind is forced to actively grapple with incongruity or contradictions.

These same researchers also found that when you're struggling with a problem, the process of ruling out possibilities is a beneficial way of getting to the answer. Participants were shown groups of words with missing letters, such as "s_eaker," which might be "sneaker" or "speaker." Some people were given a positive clue—"tennis shoe"—and invited to figure out the blank letter. Others were shown a negative clue—"not part of a stereo." The result? Participants were more apt to recall words when given a negative clue that required them to eliminate certain answers in their thought process: *Okay, it's not part of a stereo . . . so it's not "speaker." It must be "sneaker"!*

Lead researcher Sal Soraci explained, "This method of learning using negative cues is similar to how we find our way when we're driving our cars and looking for a new location. If we make a wrong turn, we're much more likely to remember the correct route next time by remembering that we shouldn't go the wrong way again." Now there's a boost for those murky days in the creative process when we seem to be making lots of wrong turns—maybe we're really bolstering our creative thinking and memory!

Sometimes fuzzy thinking may be a signal that something in your unconscious is trying to bubble up to the surface of your awareness. Is an unformed idea lurking behind a heavy fog in your mind? Do you need to bring more clarity or self-reflection to your project? Or do you need to surrender to what the Buddhists call "no mind"—the state of mind that harbors no thing and no self. It's a condition of emptiness between doing and not doing, a profound letting go.

Imagine entering the unknown in a conscious state of no mind that's empty, open, and free from preconceived judgments and expectations. In this state of consciousness, no thoughts about the past or future clutter your awareness; there's no attachment to a particular outcome. I've found this meditation practice of emptying the mind helps me tremendously during nebulous phases of the creative process.

The unknown holds many gifts. When you dare to leave the safety of familiar terrain and embrace uncertainty, a bounty of creative impulses may be waiting for you. Creativity requires a willingness to take risks, a steady trust in the mysteries of the unknown, and a desire to meet the unexpected with a spirit of *yes.*

Feeling lost, foggy, or chaotic may end up being a significant portal into the next chapter of your creative journey. So instead of getting frustrated, try surrendering to the sensation by giving yourself a period of reverie or contemplation. If you're in the middle of a busy day when the fog rolls in, make a date with yourself to do some constructive daydreaming, a no-mind meditation, or maybe even take a nap.

The Mists of Sleep

Dreams provide a fascinating bridge to transfer messages and information from your unconscious imagination to your conscious mind. Have you ever awakened from a dream with a fresh insight or new solution to a problem? This is your creative process at work synthesizing the raw material of your innermost idea factories. World-renowned inventor and computer scientist Ray Kurzweil uses lucid dreaming to help him solve creative problems. Before falling asleep, he lies in bed and imagines himself giving a lecture about how he solved the problem. "This has the purpose of seeding your subconscious to influence your dreams," he says. "The most interesting thing about dreams is that you don't consider it unusual when unusual things happen, like a room floating away," he continues. "You accept this lack of logic. And that [irrational] faculty is needed for creative thinking. But you also need to be able to apply a critical faculty, because not every idea that's different and out of the box will work."

The moments before sleep are also an excellent time to quietly repeat affirmations about your creativity. Try affirming: *I am an expression of the creative intelligence of the universe, and I am open to receiving new inspiration.*

Streaming

Nebulous moments are also great opportunities to practice *streaming*, where you express an uninterrupted flow of thoughts, feelings, and images through the art form of your choice. You might choose to stream in writing, speaking, painting, acting, music, or dance. This freestyle improvisation allows you to "outflow" whatever impulses arise without stopping to think about them or censoring yourself. You'll find that some interesting and surprising themes often emerge.

I use sound, movement, and verbal streaming exercises when I work with people in my improvisational acting workshops. The continual expression of unedited impulses develops tremendous trust, freedom, confidence, and spontaneity—it's a wonderful workout for your creative imagination. If you're feeling fuzzy and unfocused, try moving freely to the rhythms of your favorite music. If you play an instrument, experiment with musical streaming. Try asking a friend to listen as you explore your thoughts through some verbal streaming, or let the vivid colors of your paints guide your brush in the creation of spontaneous images on your canvas. I find that combined movement and verbal streaming is particularly useful for writers because it helps them bypass mental blocks and engage their body impulses and kinesthetic feelings.

Photographs provide an excellent catalyst for streaming. Try doing some streaming exercises using the images in this book. There are suggestions for photo dialogues in the section entitled *Your Creativity Journal*.

CLOUD STORIES

Too Many Choices

Occasionally, there's a deeper problem dwelling beneath the haze of a murky state of mind: too many competing ideas and choices. I remember working with a student in one of my workshops who told me that her mind perpetually felt "out of focus, like a huge impressionistic painting." Rosa had difficulty finding and pursuing clear creative choices, and I noticed that she sometimes seemed a bit spacey and unmotivated. When we worked together in private coaching sessions, she had trouble committing to a particular impulse.

After I asked her to do some free-association streaming monologues on her life and goals, I watched and listened in amazement as a plethora of unfinished dreams, schemes, and plans poured out of her. She also expressed painful frustration and regret about the unfinished condition of her numerous ideas.

We realized that Rosa's hazy mannerisms and lack of focus were cover-ups for the real problem: She was terrified of bringing creative impulses to the manifestation and completion stage. When I asked what she most feared, Rosa said she dreaded the possibility that she might be disappointed by the final outcome of her great ideas. She was unconsciously preventing herself from making clear choices because she was afraid that she wouldn't know how to develop them successfully. So rather than feel plagued by one more terrific idea that went nowhere, she hid behind a vacant persona.

During one of our sessions, I asked Rosa to pick something in nature's process of change that attracted her. She immediately said that she enjoyed driving in heavy rain and looking out the window at the passing scenery. I invited her to do a written streaming exercise on the theme of driving in a rainstorm. She wrote with great excitement as she described how everything looked like a melting painting through the watery veil of rain. She added that she especially loved the beautiful quality of calm that comes after a big storm. She'd pull over by the side of the road to experience the fresh smells of the recent rain, the sound of birds chirping, and the brilliant rainbow that often appears in the skies of the Southwest where she lives.

The moments after the end of a storm were her favorite part of the experience. I was fascinated by what she wrote because it revealed a vivid clue about her struggles with creativity. Her attraction to seeing the world through the blurry windshield of a car moving through a downpour was a vivid metaphor for her creative process. Her affinity for this rainy, impressionistic view reflected her inner landscape, where one creative impulse merged into another, and specific details were lost.

Whenever she embarked on a new creative journey, her visibility was blurred by the torrent of ideas washing over her. Her strong desire to encounter the end of the storm reflected her yearning to see her creative ideas yield satisfying results. It was no accident that Rosa was enlivened by the crisp, fresh clarity that comes after the rain.

When I shared these insights with her, she felt comforted and hopeful. We agreed that our new focus would be to help her discover how to navigate successfully in her creative storms. I was struck that she felt no fear about driving in heavy rain, and invited her to view her creative process in the same way. We used this metaphor to help her envision a satisfying, positive outcome for her creative work.

Slowly but surely, she worked on choosing *one* specific idea that she'd commit to nurture all the way to its completion. I encouraged her to lower the stakes in her mind. If she didn't like the result, she could try another approach or move on to another concept—but only *after* she'd finished the first one. I invited her to accept completion as a vital stage in the creative process that would give her an opportunity to appreciate the beautiful calm after her "storms" of doubt. She began to realize that her excellent concepts deserved the solid promise of skillful execution.

Nothing can be more disappointing than a collection of unrealized great ideas huddling like homeless orphans in the back alleys of our minds. Ironically, by avoiding the development of her ideas, Rosa was unwittingly inviting the feeling she most feared: disappointment. As we worked together on this goal of manifesting her creative impulses, her fuzzy exterior eventually dropped away. She became increasingly open to making choices and following through with them. A confident, decisive, and bright creative spirit began to emanate from her.

Rosa's willingness to learn how to manifest her ideas through concrete actions spilled over into the rest of her life. She became more adept at making and attaining career and life goals. As she let go of the hazy persona she'd previously used to protect herself from failure, she became increasingly successful. Her creative process had provided a practical container for personal development. Rosa had allowed nature to be her ultimate creativity guru by providing her with a perfect metaphor for change.

How has nature been your creativity guru? Are there natural phenomena that give meaning to your process? Have you encountered the fog of creativity? What ideas or impulses are percolating behind those mists? When you look at your creative project in the context of our larger universe, sometimes the scale of your problems and hurdles snaps into a more realistic and manageable perspective. Look for metaphors in nature that give you inspiration for your current life themes or creative yearnings. Take time to observe the details of places or living beings in nature. As Georgia O'Keeffe said, "When you take a flower in your hand and really look at it, it's your world for the moment."

INNER LIGHT

chapter 12

Structure and Improvisation

*"Making the simple complicated is
commonplace; making the complicated simple,
awesomely simple, that's creativity."*

— Charles Mingus

The ability to work with structure and the capacity to improvise are both vital in the creative process. Many people feel a greater affinity to one or the other of these skills. The goal is to become facile in both dimensions of creativity.

Learning how to understand and follow a structure is important for developing mastery as an artist. Structure is the foundation that supports your vision. It's the framework or system that organizes your work. In acting, the script is a structure that suggests specific actions and provides the actor with a blueprint for the character's life and plot. Gourmet chefs play with recipes, and fashion designers work with patterns. When you're using a structure, the creativity comes from your unique way of interpreting and adapting the outline.

Structure also enables you to learn the particular vocabulary of an art form. For example, as you become familiar with the language of knitting patterns, you become more skillful at deciphering the methods for making elaborate garments. Structure also implies practice—and the more you practice, the more proficient you become. Musicians play patterns of notes and chords to practice their technique; singers cultivate vocal dexterity by singing vocal scales in preparation for performances. The conscious repetition of these note progressions develops freedom and accurate placement. Writers hone their craft by mastering the elements of style and composition. Every art form has its own structure or pattern for you to practice.

What is your relationship to structure? Do you regard it as confining or liberating? Remember that the invention of a new structure can be innovative. The evolution of blues and jazz created new musical structures. Structure requires discipline to master the fundamentals of your art. You can't break out of a traditional structure until you have a deep understanding of the basics. It's okay to bend the rules once you know how to play the game. Studying your craft, taking classes, working as an apprentice, and of course, practicing regularly, are the first steps.

How do you feel about practicing? Do you see it as a chore or a satisfying meditation? What will motivate you to build creative practice into your daily schedule? Each time you return to your practice, you're affirming that you take yourself and your artistry seriously. Keep in mind that there's plenty of room for flexibility. Sometimes people believe that "real" practice has to be a long, laborious endeavor. Even a short period of focus on your technique can yield results. I know a singer who does her vocal exercises while she washes the dishes. By doing her scales for 20 minutes a day for ten months, she was able to add another octave to her range.

As you become adept with the tools of your art form, you'll acquire the confidence to bring more spontaneity to your investigations. You'll feel free to take more risks as you experiment with variations and innovations. Improvising without a set structure is creating without a net. Some people are stimulated by this approach, while others find it a bit scary. When we create without a preconceived pattern, we're returning to our childhood experience of coloring outside the lines. As a child, we may have been taught to stay inside the lines in order to make a neat picture. This important ability develops focus, coordination, and clarity. But we can also benefit greatly from daring to explore outside the lines.

When we venture beyond the prescribed borders, we enter the realm of improvisation. In this domain, possibilities abound. Our imagination is free to envision, invent, and discover; and the unexpected becomes a trusted friend who loves to offer us a delicious picnic of ideas.

Improvisation is an embrace of the moment. When we improvise, we feast on the offerings of each moment as we boldly imagine what might be possible. Improvisation is the art of the unknown and the science of the unexpected; it's about making choices and daring to give those choices your fullest commitment, even before you know why or where the decision will take you. Curiosity and trust fuel the engines of improvisation.

Creativity is a series of improvisational experiments. The concept of trial and error is the cornerstone of original thinking in every field. The notions of right and wrong or good and bad aren't relevant to experimentation. We don't say "trial and perfection" or "trial and success." Artists and scientists understand that errors and miscalculations often bring about insights, learning, and breakthroughs.

For example, Hubble's big discovery about the expanding universe brought to light a possible boo-boo by another creative thinker. Albert Einstein's extraordinary findings about the relationship between matter, space, time, and gravity forever changed the fields of physics, cosmology, and astronomy. But when he was developing his general theory of relativity in the early 1900s, Einstein noticed that the theory contradicted his (and other scientists') long-held assumption that the universe is a static place. In order to make his calculations comply with the notion of a static universe, he added a term called the "cosmological constant" to his equation.

Einstein called this "the greatest blunder of my life" after Hubble's new work appeared several years later. He realized that the conception of a static universe was unnecessary. One of the most distinguished geniuses of the 20th century had to rethink and modify his theory. I find it helpful to remember that story whenever I make an artistic choice that leads me offtrack.

But would we refute the rest of Einstein's enormous body of innovative work because of one misstep? I don't think so. On the contrary, his process inspires us to appreciate the dramatic importance of keeping our minds open to possibilities that might *seem* impossible at first glance. The idea of an expanding universe had seemed impossible to everyone, including Einstein. He later quipped, "Once you can accept the universe as matter expanding into nothing that is something, wearing stripes with plaid comes easy."

Ironically, recent findings have suggested that Einstein's cosmological constant may turn out to be useful now that astronomers have detected that the universe's expansion is actually speeding up, rather than slowing down. This unanticipated discovery has made Einstein's original concept relevant again. What a remarkable reminder for every creative explorer: Don't be too quick to permanently discard your earlier drafts and experiments since the future may hold an unexpected use for previously abandoned ideas.

The creative mind thrives in a nonjudgmental atmosphere of freedom and experimentation. You might try developing your creativity by intentionally going outside your comfort zone. Think of it as a practice. If following patterns is easy for you, try improvising. If improvising is your instinctive preference, try working with a structure in order to cultivate discipline and technique. Eventually, you'll find that creativity thrives within a balance of structure *and* improvisation. Departing from your comfort zone is an excellent way to expand your skills, since it catalyzes your brain to forge new neuropathways for learning.

Many people have the mistaken notion that improvising means "anything goes," but nothing could be further from the truth. It's a rigorous art of selectivity that requires a solid foundation in the skills of your craft or art form. A sophisticated improviser relies tremendously on a well-developed inner editor who isn't afraid to make specific choices: Which impulses to follow? For how long? Which ones to let go? When is it time for a new idea?

Each decision is a fertile experiment that helps you stretch your creative vision and sharpen your ultimate design. A jazz musician uses a keen understanding of music theory as a springboard for spontaneous inventions. An improvisational actor relies on an understanding of scene structure and plot development. An abstract expressionist begins with the principles of form, balance, and color in painting.

Artful improvisation ultimately creates its own structure. Clothing designer Lee Andersen has a saying: "Once a mistake; twice a problem; three times a design." From the beginning of time, humans have created rhythms, drumbeats, chants, and dances that are composed of regular accents and set configurations. The heartbeat probably provided the first prototype for music. But if some members of the tribe hadn't dared to deviate from the original rhythmic patterns, music might never have evolved from the single beat of a drum. In writing, the beat is the word; in knitting, the beat is the stitch; in theater, the beat is the dramatic action; in poetry, the beat is the syllable; and in dance, the beat is the gesture or step. The creativity comes from what you dare to do with those beats.

Your experiments with improvisation and structure are the heartbeats of your creative process. Each time you take a risk to try something new or invent a framework for your ideas, you're strengthening the pulse of your creativity. As you create, feel the steady rhythms of imagination that have inspired the human spirit throughout history. Remember that you're part of an unending expression of life's exquisite possibilities!

STAGE PRESENCE

chapter 13

Have Fun!

"If you obey all the rules, you miss all the fun!"
— Katharine Hepburn

I'd like to leave you with a final thought about creativity:
The most important ingredient for success is your ability to
have fun. Remember to enjoy yourself. Remember to play.
Without joy, your work will soon feel tedious and meaningless. I'm convinced that the joy of creation is what ultimately
motivates and sustains us. Roll up your sleeves and dive into
your favorite creative sandbox with enthusiasm and delight.
Bring your humor with you when you're trying to climb over
seemingly insurmountable obstacles.

Remember that life is short, and in the context of cosmic
time, we're here for the weekend! Here are a few tips I've
learned along the way:

- Take risks, experiment, and don't be afraid to make
  a fool of yourself.

- Make sure to mix in some pleasure breaks during
  times of intense work.

- Be bold and audacious.

- Say yes to the unexpected.

- Make friends with failure.

- Make friends with success.

- Gather a community of positive support around you.

- Remember that creativity thrives in friendship and collaboration.

- Strive for excellence without trying to be perfect.

- Cherish the process—especially while you're in the middle of it.

- Don't get too attached to outcomes, but appreciate what comes out.

- Face your demons.

- Remember that your every creative act is part of something much bigger.

- When in doubt, ask for help.

- Learn new skills regularly.

- Play often and with gusto.

- Congratulate yourself when you notice that you've acquired mastery.

- Let your imagination run free.

- When things go wrong, look for a laugh instead of a noose.

- Remember that your current creative project is there to lead you to the next one.

- Fill up with the food of satisfaction when you achieve the results you seek.

- Find delight in the journey!

INVITATION

Now that we've explored the power of the creative process as a path of self-awareness, let's apply these insights to the contemplative practice of knitting. Let's look at knitting as a metaphor for life.

PART II

Knitting as a Metaphor for Life

by Wren Ross

chapter 14

Why Knit? Why Knot?

"The stitch is lost unless the thread be knotted."
— Italian proverb

Celebrities, dignitaries, sports heroes, men, women, and children have all been seen recently with balls of yarn and needles. Groups are being formed throughout the world dedicated to sitting, chatting, and knitting. People love the way it makes them feel. Knitting has been called the "new yoga." Why? Both yoga and knitting are relaxing, and both are practices that help one focus and be mindful. But the similarity goes further: The word *yoga* means "union." It's the connection between mind and body, and knitting is all about connection, knot by knot.

Why knit? Why knot? The answer lies in the knots themselves. Knitting is a process of making a series of knots or loops that are intertwined to create a fabric. The word *knitting* comes from the Old English word *cnyttan:* to tie in a knot. Early knitting was thought to be a primitive technique of making loops called "needle netting" or nalbinding.

Knots are powerful symbols of birth, death, love, safety, freedom, and infinity. Besides advancing civilized life by being practical in countless ways, they've been used as protection, to cast magical spells, and even as language throughout the centuries. Today, mathematicians investigate knot theory and its far-reaching impact on chemistry, physics, psychology, and molecular biology. Knots may hold the key to understanding the universe.

We come into the world attached by a cord, and our first amulet of life is a knot in our navel, our very center. As children, learning to tie a knot on our shoes was a rite of passage symbolizing independence and a newfound ability to stand on our own two feet. When we're getting married, we "tie the knot" to create a lifelong bond. Stress manifests knots in our muscles that let us know we need to unwind. When we die, we untie the knot that connects us to our material bodies.

Knots are symbols that represent the profound dualities of the human experience. Within one symbol, knots can represent the seemingly contradictory forces of birth and death, freedom and union. We can untie knots to release, and tie them to unite. The very words *unite* and *untie* have a bond: They're both composed of the same five letters, and their meanings may change by merely switching the *i* and *t* within the word.

Knitting is calming. Just watch people knit: A reflective look softens their faces, and their hands look to be in prayer. Each knot becomes a mantra, a repeated sacred phrase, much like using rosaries, Buddhist prayer beads, or the fringes of the Jewish prayer shawl. The rhythmic click of the needles is a way to quiet the mind, hear thoughts, and find inner peace.

Dr. Herbert Benson of the Mind/Body Medical Institute at Harvard University and author of *The Relaxation Response* says, "Working with yarn provides stress relief: Like meditation or prayer, knitting allows for the passive release of stray thoughts. The rhythmic and repetitive quality of the stitching, along with the needles clicking, resembles a calming mantra." When we perform repetitive motions such as knitting, the hormone noradrenaline is blocked, which lowers blood pressure and heart rate. This produces a soothing state of mind.

Dr. Susan Taylor, an expert in nutritional biochemistry, meditation, and yoga comments, "Concentration on an activity that requires us to use both hands, provides focus. It's the *focus* that produces the relaxation of knitting." Each stitch is a breath, a moment, an opportunity to send healing and positive intentions to ourselves, someone we love, or even a stranger. There's something *holy* about making a *whole* project from stitches that have *holes* in their center.

Knitting is rich with life metaphors: We become "unraveled"; they're a "close-knit" group; he's a "dyed-in-the-wool" idealist; and she's all "tangled up." The snags and flows of living can be mirrored in the process of working with fiber—fiber is how we measure the substance and character of something or someone. If the fibers in a straw basket have integrity and strength, they will carry your heaviest load. The wool fibers of an Aran fisherman's sweater were made to withstand the wear and tear of the sea. We see how strong a person's moral fiber is when they're in extreme circumstances or under pressure.

Thread is the symbol of life itself. Think of the mythological Fates whose purpose was to spin, measure, and cut the thread of life. We're the creator of our own life's fabric, using our hands, heart, mind, and imagination. Our very essence—DNA—is composed of strands that make us who we are. Fiber is indeed the stuff of life.

The Sanskrit word *sutra* means "thread" or "string," and refers to a practice or narrative. In her book *The Knitting Sutra,* Susan Gordon Lydon said, "Our connections to one another are sacred, as all life is sacred, as all of the earth is sacred; the circle that winds around the earth forms the hoop that is also sacred." Buddhist sutras are dialogues with Buddha. Yoga sutra is the daily dialogue between our mind, body, and spirit in the exercise of yoga poses. Sutras are practices that connect threads in our lives.

Knitting, too, may be used as a sutra for self-growth and inner dialogue. It teaches us about our relationship to beginnings (casting on) and endings (binding off), how we become unraveled or get into tangles, and how we can deal with our mistakes. We may learn to distinguish when a mistake is a new pattern or opportunity, and when we need to rip out a mistake and begin again. While knitting, we may learn the nitty-gritty of life by listening to the message of metaphor. I call this "fiber philosophy."

There's a theory in physics that seeks to unify the forces of nature called "string theory." It postulates that the essence of every atom consists of vibrating string. Well, if that's so, then the whole universe is an amazingly complex afghan! It's reassuring and inspiring to share the same hobby with creation itself. Using two sticks and some yarn, we're making something that wasn't there before.

Knitting transforms the ordinary into the extraordinary. It's art in everyday life. Practical items such as a hat, sweater, baby blanket, or gloves are elevated because of the love and time knitted into each stitch.

Knitting is a creative playground that allows us to exercise our mental and physical dexterity. It has a basic language of two stitches, knit and purl, from which a multitude of patterns and designs can be made. Studies have shown that the brain stays young by learning new skills that utilize its left and right sides. When we knit, we use both the right hemisphere (intuitive and creative) and left hemisphere (logical and analytical) parts of our brain, so there's much benefit to be derived when mastering a new cable or lace pattern.

The Waldorf schools are innovative private institutions that teach knitting to their first-graders because it gives children dexterity, concentration skills, and practical math training. If knitting can teach young people geometry, algebra, and color appreciation and help them focus, perhaps it can be an effective remedy for hyperactivity and the restlessness we find in children today. Why not encourage them to knit?

The language of knitting is universal. No matter what our country of origin or native tongue, we can communicate through the kinesthetic concepts of knitting and purling. The unique culture of knitting crosses all boundaries of sex, age, class, race, politics, culture, or religion. I was impressed by this diversity when I was invited to sing at the New York City Knit-Out & Crochet event. Everyone was deeply absorbed and full of enthusiasm as they traded hints and stories about knitting. My favorite pair was a young transgendered man wearing a bright-red boa and four-inch heels who was teaching a new stitch to an elderly African-American grandmother. They were laughing together and totally enthralled in the stitch of the moment. Casting on leaves no room for intolerance.

Knitting creates community. There's an old tradition of people meeting together in knitting circles to spin yarns figuratively and literally. When people knit together, they share secrets, techniques, laughter, and find a soothing hand-to-hand comfort. It's common for these groups to contribute some of their work to charity . . . and the fabric of life is made brighter and stronger.

Knitting is optimistic. My "stash" bins, filled with gorgeous yarns of every color and texture, are the ultimate representation of hope for the future. Others may see mounds of yarn in the bin, but I see sweaters, shawls, socks, and scarves.

All that fiber is representative of the potential of what can or might be. The comedian George Burns used to say, "I can't die, I'm booked." I say, "I can't die, I have stash."

Knitting says *yes* to learning, *yes* to beauty and creativity, *yes* to kindness and compassion, *yes* to peace, and *yes* to life. It does all this and has another big bonus: At the end of our knitting experience we can produce something useful and beautiful from our own hands, imagination, and time. As John Keats said, "A thing of beauty is a joy for ever." So why not knit?

PASSING IT ON

chapter 15

Knots

> *"Friendship is a knot tied by angels' hands."*
> — Anonymous

What are we doing when we knit? We're making a series of knots. It's inspiring to consider the rich and intrinsic significance of knots in human history. Here are a few examples of the meaning and symbolism of knots in various religions and cultural traditions throughout time.

TZITZIT

Kesher (קֶשֶׁר): *Kesher* is the Hebrew word for "knot"; it also means "relationship" and "networking." Knots are symbolic and significant in Judaism. Rabbi Berel Levertov of the Santa Fe Chabad told me that the knots on the fringes *(tzitzit)* of the Jewish prayer shawl *(tallit)* are similar to the knots we tie around a finger to remember something. When praying, a person may touch and kiss these knots to remember one's bond to God and to the 613 commandments that must be performed in life.

Rabbi Levertov said, "According to Kabbalah, the tallit represents the infinite Divine energy (light) that surrounds and encompasses the whole creation and everything that's in it. The strings are like strands of thin light and energy that flow down from the infinite. Strands of human hair are also called 'tzitzit.'" He went on to say, "It's a violation to tie or untie a knot on Shabbat, because tying and untying are 'creating,' which God rested from on the Shabbat, and so do we."

I enjoyed many talks with Rabbi Ben-Zion Gold, director emeritus of Harvard Hillel, who told me that for daily morning prayer one wears tefillin, which are two leather boxes that contain scriptures from Exodus and Deuteronomy. One tefillin box is placed on the forehead between the eyes, with its straps knotted in the back of the head; and the other box's straps are wrapped and knotted down the left bicep to the hand in such a way as to spell the Hebrew name of God. The word *tefillin* comes from the Hebrew root word for prayer.

I spoke with Dr. Steven B. Schram, an acupuncturist and chiropractor who has written articles published in *The Journal of Chinese Medicine* about the relationship between the knot placement of tefillin and acupuncture points in traditional Chinese medicine. Dr. Schram said, "The acknowledged purpose of the tefillin is to raise the spiritual consciousness of those who wear it. If we examine where the knots and wrappings are placed from a traditional Chinese medicine point of view, it appears that the tefillin and wraps form a potent acupuncture point formula focused on the spinal cord centers that nourish the brain and aim to elevate the spirit and clear the mind."

In Jewish burial preparation, narrow sashes are wrapped around the head, ankles, and waist with loops forming the letter *shin* representing God's name; the loops face the heart of the deceased. Those who perform ritual burial purification are called Chevra Kadisha, which means "Holy Society." I was told that members of Chevra Kadisha are very careful *not* to make knots in the sashes, but rather loops that easily slide out, since knots represent permanence. Death isn't permanent—the spirit of the deceased lives on. These loops are described as "slipknots," the same ones that we use when casting on a row of knitting. Our knitting isn't permanent either: At any time we may unravel a sweater and transform it into another garment—we might think of this as knitting reincarnation.

KHIPU

Khipu: The Inca culture had knotted string devices called *khipus,* which is the word for *knot* in the ancient language of Peru. Khipus functioned as tools to communicate and record Inca heritage. Each knot, twist, and color, as well the choice of fiber and how it was attached, had meaning and a message. The khipu knots could be read as a language. Gary Urton of Harvard University, who has researched khipu extensively, wrote a book called *Signs of the Inka Khipu* that explores the theory that the knots form a binary code similar to that used in computer programming.

All knitted garments have a language. In the beginning of the craft, there were no written patterns. Instead, a knitter would learn to "read" the stitches. In this way, patterns would be passed down through generations, and oral history merged with tactile tradition. Many illiterate knitters created intricate lace, cables, and color work that spoke volumes.

BUDDHIST ETERNAL KNOT

Buddhist Eternal Knot: I had some great conversations with my Tibetan friend Ngodup Sangpo who told me many interesting things about knots in Buddhism. This symbol depicted in the illustration is called *srivatsa* in Sanskrit. It represents the infinite interconnection of all things and is one of the eight auspicious symbols in Buddhism. Srivatsa symbolizes the wisdom of Buddha and eternal life without beginning or end. Upon untying the infinite knot under the Bodhi tree, Buddha found enlightenment.

Tibetan Buddhists put a knot on a doorpost to provide a shield from the winds of bad fortune. The knotted tassel at the end of the Buddhist mala prayer beads is also intended to offer protection, as it's believed that evil spirits do not like dangling objects. The tassel has nine knots to signify the nine energy centers of the body.

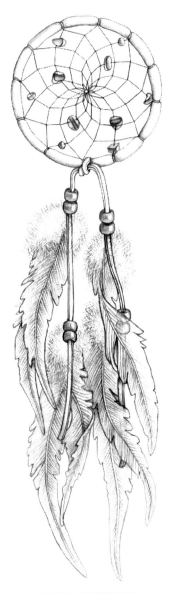

DREAMCATCHER

Dreamcatcher: A dreamcatcher is a Native American tool made of a flexible, circular piece of wood that's filled in with a net of knotted string. Its purpose is to filter bad dreams into the net and let good ones pass through.

Prayer ties: LaRayne Willard of St. Joseph's Indian School told me about a beautiful tradition in the Lakota culture of making knotted prayer ties. The Lakota people collect cloth that is meaningful to them—it could be a light cotton cloth that is not bulky, and the colors are often red, white, black, yellow, purple, green, or blue depending on the ceremony. They tear the cloth into squares to form a pouch and put a pinch of sacred tobacco into the center. These pouches are then tied together with yarn or string while chanting prayers. Prayers can be said silently, as well as sung or chanted. When finished, the prayer ties can be hung in many different places, depending upon the ceremony or purpose for making them: on a buffalo skull, in a prayer lodge, on a tree, or any high place outside. After a time, the tie is taken down and burned so that the messages imbued in the knots will be released through the smoke into the atmosphere.

CELTIC TRINITY KNOT

Celtic knots: There's an enormously rich tradition of knot designs in the Celtic culture. Used decoratively in jewelry and book illustration, these knot designs are thought to have deep symbolic resonance. It's held that the trinity knot represents the triple aspect of the goddess—maid, mother, and crone—while the labyrinth knot is representative of the journey of life.

Cincture: The Franciscan monks wear a rope around their robes called a cincture that's fastened by making three knots that symbolize their vows of poverty, chastity, and obedience. St. Francis of Assisi wore rough cords around his waist to honor the ropes that bound Jesus to the cross.

Mythological Knots

Gordian knot: There are powerful myths attached to the releasing or making of knots. The Gordian knot is a symbol for finding a dramatic and expedient way to solve a problem. Gordius, king of Phrygia in Asia Minor, tied an extremely complicated knot and predicted that whoever untied it would rule Asia. No one could find the way to undo this complicated knot until Alexander the Great cut the Gordian knot with his sword. Some contend that the reason Alexander's rule was brief was in part because the knot was meant to be disentangled, not cut by a sword.

Herculean knot: The Herculean knot is a symbol of courage and strong union. For his first heroic task, Hercules had to fight the fierce lion of Nemea. He couldn't pierce the tough hide of the lion with his sword but had to wrestle it with his bare hands and strangle it. Since the hide couldn't be penetrated by his sword, Hercules had to use the lion's own talons to skin the beast. Hercules wore the lion as a trophy and tied its paws under his chin in a square knot that got tighter when pulled. Hence the square Herculean knot has been a popular symbol in wedding rings to represent a solid and unbreakable bond.

LOVER'S KNOT

Sailors' knots: Sailors spoke with knots: When a sailor was at sea for an extended period of time, he would send his sweetheart a heart-shaped knot that was half tied. If the knot came back completed, he knew that his beloved would be his wife and was faithful. If the knot came back half-done, he knew that she was uncertain; and if it returned untied, he knew that he had to find another to love. This knot was called the lover's knot.

In times past, sailors depended upon knots for their safety and survival. One of the first skills a sailor learned was how to make hitches and knots for anchoring and making boundaries; they had to "learn the ropes."

Also, mariners measure time and distance at sea using the term *knots.* If we think of a moment as being a knot, then knitting a series of moments together creates the fabric of time.

chapter 16

Learning Is Not Knowing

*"When we have no thought of achievement,
no thought of self, we are true beginners.
Then we can really learn something . . .
This is the real secret of the arts:
always be a beginner."*

— Shunryu Suzuki

You don't need to be a knitting whiz to relate to the discussions in this book. This book is meant for everyone—experienced knitters, novices, and non-knitters alike. Making mistakes, unraveling, ripping out what isn't wanted, beginnings, and endings are life metaphors relevant to you whether you've knitted for five decades, five years, five minutes, or never at all. If you've lived on this planet as a human being, you've undoubtedly encountered these life lessons at some point. You might use any skill or art form as a life metaphor: Gardening, cooking, woodworking, or photography are all filled with profound life lessons.

I happen to love knitting and find it a great source of wisdom. My purpose is to use yarn and needles to uncover the relevant life lessons imbued in this craft. Of course, if you want to learn how to knit or learn a *new approach* to knitting in the process, that's swell, too.

Learning can be food for the mind and soul. Curiosity keeps us young and vibrant and allows us to partake of the endless bounty of the universe. In the first part of this book, Daena discussed Shunryu Suzuki's concept of *beginner's mind* as a way to approach the unknown. The experience of learning a new skill teaches us a lot about ourselves. It's important to note that beginner's mind is different from the act of beginning. Beginner's mind is a quality of flexibility and openness that you bring to all stages of an endeavor. We may even have beginner's mind when ending a project. What might happen if you bring beginner's mind to your knitting and your life?

I'm reminded of a Zen story that I saw in the book *Zen Flesh, Zen Bones* compiled by Paul Reps and Nyogen Senzaki. A young man goes to study with the wise and learned master Nan-in. The student tells Nan-in that he has read every book that the master has written in preparation for his classes. Nan-in smiles and asks if the young man would like some tea.

"Oh, yes!" says the young man. The master puts out the cups and teapot and proceeds to pour. The tea reaches the top of the cup, and Nan-in pours still more liquid until the table and floor are flooded with the overflowing tea. "Oh, master," the young man exclaims, "the teacup is filled, and you can't pour in more tea!"

"Yes, young man," says Nan-in, "that is how you have come to me today. You have come to learn, but you are a cup full of information and opinions. How can I put anything in? Come as an empty cup and I can teach you."

Learning isn't about what you know or being right. When I strain to be right, I usually mess up. That's because my intention is to be *right,* instead of simply doing what needs to be done.

Ask professional athletes, and they'll tell you that they aren't focused on how well they're doing. Rather, they're intensely involved and concentrating on the specifics of playing the game. How is the ball coming across the plate? What kind of pitches does that pitcher tend to throw? Who's on first base?

As a young singer, I started to sing well when I stopped trying to be a "good singer" and simply focused on the melody and lyrics as a way to enter the event of the song. I found my own authentic voice instead of the voice I thought I was *supposed* to have. "Right" is usually your projection of what you think *someone else* wants or expects—it has nothing to do with *your* personal expression. Being right can create a static state of mind that will produce stale, predictable results. It's far better to find a way to make something work than to get it right.

If you're fixated on whether you're learning something quickly and not looking stupid, how can you pay attention to simply watching the direction of the yarn and feeling what your hands do with the needles? How can you know something before you learn it? Osmosis? Magic? I don't think so. No wonder many people get frustrated and abandon the instructions. Learning is a step-by-step process, and like knitting, it takes time to get the task done. You can't rush it.

For some new skills, I'm a slow learner. That's not a measure of my intelligence; it's just the way I assimilate new information. When I stopped expecting myself to grasp something right away, I noticed that it was more fun to learn, and I was motivated to learn more. What a relief! I started figuring out how to please myself and not prove myself to some inner or outer critic. I also noticed that I acquired the new skill with more ease.

The Mask of Nervousness

Let's talk about pleasing people and trying to be "good enough" for someone else. We all do it. How many times have we been in situations where our main concern was someone else's approval or criticism? I suspect that the answer is too many times. It's part of our conditioning as children to please adults and do what they want and expect. Those old habits die hard.

Trying to please other people will inevitably make us frustrated, resentful, and angry. It's humiliating and hurtful to think that we have to be something special and that what we are isn't good enough. I believe that underneath all nervousness and performance anxiety is a layer of unexpressed frustration and rage. Because it's "naughty" to be in touch with feelings of anger as children, we find ways to channel those big feelings into socially acceptable behaviors. Anger has a stigma of being bad, when actually it's simply a natural reaction to feeling hurt. If I accidentally step on my cat's tail, she doesn't say, "I'm sorry that I was in the way of your foot." She hisses.

Nervousness, anxiety, depression, and feelings of insecurity are all uncomfortable emotions to experience, but they're more socially acceptable than anger. So when we're trying to please someone, our anger gets expressed indirectly, often masked as nervousness. We become self-absorbed, withdrawn, blank, shaky, and not fully ourselves. What clever and resourceful ways our psyches find to express anger!

I'm not advocating howling and lashing out with rage when you're learning something new. But if you're aware that you may be feeling nervous and insecure because you're buying into the notion that you have to be "good enough" or "right," you may be able to reverse that negative thinking, release the pressure to please, and enjoy the process of whatever you're doing. Anger becomes less destructive and overwhelming when we feel justified in our emotions.

Self-awareness is a great tool when seeking to change some of these old thought patterns. Rather than feeling weak and nervous, you can understand that you have a right to be angry in response to the hurtful message that you're not good enough. You'll feel stronger.

I also find it helpful to remember that in the end, people would rather be *appreciated* than impressed. As much as we may think that our prowess and expertise will bring us love, in the end, it's being loving that brings us love.

Persistence Is a Virtue

People always remark on my patience as a knitter. I am not patient. I hate to waste time. Why else would I knit at a stoplight or in line at the bank? However, I *am* persistent. How do we get to Carnegie Hall? Practice. Practice. Practice. Learning to knit is a great way to learn *how* to practice and stick with something. There's always more to learn in knit-ting and in life. Although we may be a little awkward at the beginning, eventually our efforts will pay off. Michelangelo said, "If you knew how hard I worked, you wouldn't call me a genius."

Knitting is the ultimate testament of persistence, since it progresses one stitch at a time. There are no shortcuts. It takes needles, yarn, skill, inspiration, and *time* to make something. A knitted garment is a chronicle that you were present while your hands touched every inch of fiber. I believe that's why we love knitted objects: We see the passage of time, intention, and effort in the hat, sweater, and afghan. A really intricate lace pattern, Aran-cable sweater, or Fair Isle pattern makes us say, "Ah!" because we appreciate how much energy it took to create the fabric.

In life, our diligence and focus always pay off, although sometimes the results are slow. When we plant the seeds for a new lawn, it may seem as if the grass is taking forever to grow. But before we know it, we *will* have to mow that lawn. *The I Ching* or *Book of Changes* says: "Persistence furthers." The tapestry of life is created one breath, one step, one stitch at a time.

OPTIMISM

chapter 17

Casting On

*"The journey of a thousand
miles begins with a single step."*

— Lao Tzu

In our case, the journey of a thousand knitted projects starts with one stitch. Beginning or creating a foundation of knots for knitting is called *casting on.*

How do we cast on? Let me count the ways: There are more than 40 different ways to cast on and over 40 different definitions for the word *cast.* We can cast a mold, cast a fishing line, cast an actor to play a role, cast a darting glance, or cast a ballot—just to name a few. In knitting, there are many methods for casting on: long tail, cable, knitted, crochet, provisional, and so on. There are so many different ways to begin!

How we begin is crucial in knitting—and in life as well. Why? It's our foundation. In knitting, if we cast on too tightly, it will be difficult to make stitches, and they may even break.

In life, we know people who have a tendency to begin an endeavor with so much rigid overplanning that the enterprise

169

never has a chance to get off the ground. There's no spirit left in the project after all that fretting and fussing.

Conversely, casting on too loosely creates a sloppy edge that will result in a misshapen garment. And how often have we haphazardly thrown ourselves into a situation without thinking, only to find that we didn't have the basic tools to ensure success? Slipshod event planning can result in an unorganized and unsatisfying experience.

Beginnings need both the precise care of casting a mold and the optimistic and enthusiastic freedom of casting a fishing line. And just as there are different methods for fishing, depending upon the situation, there are many different ways to cast on a knitting project. As with any beginning, assess what you require: Do you need a firm or decorative edge? Do you want to add more stitches later? Will the garment flow or be immobile?

Beginning is a process that's marked by an act of initiation called starting. It's the moment you cast on, the first pitch of the ball game, or the first day of college. Beginnings may be emotionally charged. Some people experience dread and doubt, while others will be joyful and hopeful when embarking on a new endeavor.

Beginnings are often litmus tests of your beliefs. Do you expect to fail? Do you feel that the project has to be perfect in order to be satisfying? Do you anticipate that you'll be bored, or imagine that the new endeavor will be problematic? Do you begin with unrealistic expectations? Do you start recklessly without care or thought?

Your *intention* when beginning anything in life is what's most important. An open mind and a strong, positive intention will ensure a good outcome. When beginning to knit, it's most important to have an open, curious, and optimistic mind—and this attitude is essential no matter what new skill you undertake. Knitting is merely making a series of knots with two sticks. If you've learned to tie your shoes, you'll be able to knit.

Without judgment, try to witness your thought patterns and expectations as you learn to knit. Are you easily frustrated? Are you comparing yourself to someone who's knitted for years? Try to observe these thoughts without getting sucked into a vortex of negativity. Those ideas are just pesky flies that are trying to distract you from the tasty lunch of learning that's in front of you. Stay focused on your hands, the needles, and the yarn, and just learn one step at a time.

You may begin by thinking, *I'm never going to get this.* But eventually that thought will dissipate, and the new skill will become second nature. There's an old saying that "confusion is the halfway house to wisdom." Try not to have overly high expectations or attachments to success. Be as kind and patient to yourself as you would be to a five-year-old just learning this new skill. Your effort is a triumph in itself.

Get help if you need it. If you have trouble learning from directions and charts in books, seek instruction by finding a knitting group or a friendly local yarn store. There's something timeless in the way this craft has been passed down hand-to-hand for generations. You'll learn more quickly with wise guides nearby, and may find new friends in the process . . . and receiving encouragement is invaluable.

Asking for help is also a necessary life skill. We can't do everything alone, and there's no shame in asking someone for assistance with a problem. In fact, it's generous to ask for suggestions or advice, since helping others puts a deposit of "goodwill" in the friendship bank. When we do, we're letting our "helpers" know that we respect and value them. Everyone wants to feel useful.

STILL STANDING

If we can learn positive and effective new ways to begin, we may find more self-confidence and strength in all that we do. Casting on can be a powerful act of personal transformation if we endow our beginning with positive affirmations and actions. As Plato said, "The beginning is the most important part of the work."

Beginning and "Start-itis"

I know a woman named Judith who loves beginnings so much that she's developed a condition that fellow knitters refer to as "start-itis." Sometimes Judith has 20 projects on the needles at a time. Although start-itis is creative and fun, it can also be overwhelming—Judith told me that she often feels like a shepherd tending a flock of projects. She spends so much time debating which one to work on that she doesn't work on anything at all.

Start-itis is encouraged by our culture through the constant advertising that insists we should acquire more of everything. We're supposed to be in a constant state of doing, going, and getting. Our music videos jump from image to image, and our brains barely register one idea before another replaces it. We are overstimulated. It's no wonder why so many people—especially children—are diagnosed with attention deficit disorder these days—there's way too much information to digest. When babies are overwhelmed with too many faces cooing, toys rattling, and mobiles flapping, they express their distress by crying. It isn't healthy to have excessive stimulation.

I asked Judith what purpose start-itis serves in her psyche. She thought for a while and then wondered if the distraction of many projects was her way to deal with competition and expectation in her life. Judith comes from a highly ambitious and successful academic family: Her father is a famous mathematician, her mother is a noted linguist, and her sister is an accomplished lawyer. Being "the best" was a big theme as she grew up. Although she's a successful advertising executive full of brilliant ideas, she never feels that she measures up. Her family loves to make jokes about her knitting and refers to it as her "little hobby."

Judith's overabundant unfinished projects reflect her desperation to impress her family. Ironically, starting a lot of things simultaneously prevents her from taking her creative work—and herself—seriously. How can she be fully present in the moment and paying attention to the details that ensure excellence when she's frenzied with the distraction of 20 projects?

In fact, Judith's "start-itis" is a symptom of her secret desire to take herself out of the family achievement contest and *not* compete. She conveniently avoids the pressure of excelling on her family's terms by not completing projects. How can she win or lose if she never finishes anything?

I saw Judith recently and noticed that her usually bulging knitting bag was lighter. She told me that our discussion about her start-itis had a profound effect: She realized that she needed to define achievement on her own terms and not her family's, so she decided to start her knitting projects with more consciousness and a clear commitment to developing just a few of them at a time. With more focus, Judith found greater pleasure in her creative process and knitting.

STARTING POINT

chapter 18

Knitter's Mind

"When it's over, I want to say: all my life
I was a bride married to amazement. I was the
bridegroom, taking the world into my arms."

— Mary Oliver

K nitting has taught me many lessons, but the one I most value is enjoyment. I love to knit, and it seems as if I've always knit. I can't remember exactly when I began. Sometimes I think that when I was born, I began casting on with my umbilical cord! However, I suspect that it was when I was a Brownie or Girl Scout that I got my first knitting lesson. I've seen evidence of this on my green Girl Scout sash, which has a prominent badge featuring needles and a ball of yarn.

When I was little, I made marvelous purple-acrylic garter-stitch wrappings for my Barbie doll. And, of course, there was that brown and maize, ridiculously long and holey scarf for the first boyfriend. Eventually, as I developed expertise, I learned to design sweaters. Today, some of my favorite projects are floor-length coats with a multitude of colors and symbols that chronicle my life. I call these wearable altars "Stories of Fiber."

I adore knitting. Some who are jaded by our cynical, apathetic "whatever" culture may call this an obsession. I call it passion. I believe it's vital for everyone on the planet to have a passion for *something*—it could be dogs, photography, dancing, sailing, or the study of fleas. Passion gives us a reason to wake up in the morning and something to dream about at night. It calls on us to be the most "us" that we can be: curious, focused, persistent, and hungry to grow and improve. Passion also provides a haven from the challenges of the world. This refuge is a place to find purpose and be absorbed. I call my passionate knitting sanctuary "Knitter's Mind."

Knitter's Mind is more than love for fiber or the great sense of accomplishment when I've finished with a project. Knitter's mind is a special kind of inner peace. There's a quiet diffusion in the mind produced by the repetitious flow of stitches and the tapping of the needles . . . the alpha waves line up in a happy way.

When our minds focus, they release tightness, and a calm emerges that allows us to hear our own thoughts. In most meditation practices, we repeat a mantra or focus on the breath to quiet the mind. While knitting, our hands do the repetitious work, allowing a vast horizon to appear inside our head.

Opening that space in my mind lets new thoughts and perspectives emerge. I've found countless solutions for seemingly insurmountable challenges while knitting, and I've been amused by forgotten memories that float into my head. I've even written songs about the delights and dilemmas of being a "knitaholic" while knitting.

Knitter's Mind is a respite from to-do lists. My inner drill sergeant appears when I do just about anything. I could be cooking, singing a beautiful song, or walking on the treadmill, and my drill sergeant scolds me, telling me that I'm doing the wrong thing. I *should* be doing my taxes, returning calls, writing this chapter, or learning to skydive.

When I knit, I knit; I don't want to do anything else. A knitter is always happy knitting—unless she's a designer with a deadline, and then she'd rather be knitting something else for herself! A knitter's motto is: "One more row."

It's a paradox that too often we fail to *enjoy* the things we love to do. Tyrannical puritanical guilt about what we think we *ought* to be doing crowds our minds, or we get obsessed with the illusion of perfection. Maybe some deadline is looming over our heads. We often need permission to enjoy ourselves.

Try knitting for knitting's sake, writing for writing's sake, or washing the dishes just to wash the dishes. Even if we have only ten minutes to knit, we can make each moment count by being fully present and enjoying ourselves. I believe that people who are driven to be successful often don't have fun, but people who are having fun are often successful. Sometimes creating the process by which we work is as creative as the work itself. When our intention is to be joyfully absorbed in the process, the product is often excellent.

The key to Knitter's Mind is being intimately at one with something we love, not because we'll reap rewards from it, but simply because it makes us feel good. What do you love to do? What inspires you?

If we love to do something, we find motivation, concentration, and persistence. We learn and master the skill, and feel productive and alive. If we develop a taste for relishing each moment with a hobby or creative artistic endeavor, we can transfer that delight to all aspects of our life.

A Haven of Beauty and Comfort

I love yarn shops. Whether it's a booth at a farmers' market, an exotic bazaar in a foreign land, a factory-warehouse outlet, the living room of a friendly spinner, or the local store where everyone knows your name, yarn shops are temples of creative possibility. They're the hearth and hub of knitting life.

In the old days, there used to be a plaza or town square where everyone would gather. This was where it all happened: People would meet and greet; buy and sell; and trade secrets, stories, gossip, and advice. They'd fall in and out of love. They'd learn new things.

Now, we spend so much time staring at computers inside cubicles or isolated in our cars that we crave community. The yarn shop has become the new town plaza. It's the place to see and be seen, show and be shown: "Look at the poncho I finished with this fabulous bamboo yarn!" "Wow, I love the way your colors work on that baby blanket." "How's your Aran sweater coming along?"

I'm not the only knitter whose heart quickens when crossing the threshold of a yarn store. I feel energized and stimulated—there's so much beauty to behold and envision. These shops are cornucopias of color and texture. Each skein of yarn has a siren call that promises a scarf for your sister, a pair of socks for a friend, a sweater for Dad, and a felted bag for yourself.

I never look at my watch in a yarn shop. I'm so absorbed and happy that time flies by. I must admit that I've gotten a few parking tickets because of this passion, but it's a small price for ecstasy.

Yarn stores can be a great source of exercise for knitters. Although knitting may be a sedentary activity, when you're at a yarn store, there are countless opportunities to flex your muscles. You can stretch repeatedly to get the lovely gray alpaca on the top shelf or bend and squat when admiring the pink-cotton tweed in the basket on the floor. Sometimes you can even get an aerobic workout if you're really excited about the yarn and need to jump up and down!

Yarn stores are universities. Many of them offer classes or informal drop-in lessons where you can learn to your heart's content and acquire new skills. Each new skill gives you the ability to knit a more complex project. You can graduate from a scarf to a shawl; eventually, you'll be ready for a sweater. And there are so many different ways to learn the same thing: If you knit Continental style by "picking" the yarn, you can learn to "throw" using the English wrapping method. Knitting is basically easy, but it can also provide challenges when you're ready. It's never boring. Knitting provides unlimited brain food.

A yarn store is a place dedicated to connection. The art of knitting is bringing fiber together to make a fabric. People from every corner of life come to yarn shops and find that they can knit together despite their differences—old and young, men and women, conservative and liberal, gay and straight, rich and poor. All ethnic, religious, and cultural groups commingle. They're bonded together by the stitches of a common love. They're friends of fiber.

A yarn store is a sanctuary for me. No matter what my state of mind might be when I enter, I know that I'll feel refreshed and renewed when I leave. Everybody needs a sanctuary and a teeming town plaza in life. What's yours?

NEEDLE MANIA

chapter 19

Knitting as a Meditative and Contemplative Craft

*"Artisans maintain the fabric of the world,
and in the handiwork of their craft is their prayer."*
— Ben Sira

The original knitters were thought to be nomadic Arab shepherds sitting in the fields using string and their fingers to make nets and socks. They carried their work around with them, and so do I. Much of my knitting is usually crammed into a plastic grocery bag and left near the couch or stuffed in my purse. I love knitting because it's portable peace of mind. I take my projects almost everywhere. That's why knitters love to wait: We're never fazed when a meeting is delayed or a doctor is late, because at least we can finish that hat.

There are as many reasons and ways to knit as there are knitters. Some people knit in groups, finding comfort from conversation and connection, while some knit to relax and take their minds off their problems. There are different projects that suit inner need and outer necessity. We may want to knit a simple shawl or afghan when in social situations so that

KNITTING MEDITATION

we don't lose our place; a mindless scarf is soothing because life is too complicated, and we crave simplicity. We might want an intricate cable or color pattern when we crave a challenge. Socks can be perfect for travel since they're small and easy to transport. Most knitters have more than one project on the needles at a time.

Over the years, I've found that in addition to being fun, practical, and portable, knitting may also serve as a profound tool to change the fabric of my being. There are projects that I don't tote around in public and times that I don't talk or watch TV while knitting. I use knitting as a form of meditation and ritual. Since doing this practice, I've found more peace, insight, and love in my life.

Here's what I do: I wash my hands and then go to a specific corner of my office that's my "personal place," where I light a candle. I use special yarn and needles placed in a beautiful container. I carve time for myself—anywhere from five minutes to an hour—to knit consciously, using affirmations that address personal issues as well as express gratitude. I knit with intention.

Knitting Intentions

Intentions are powerful agents of change. They're the conscious or unconscious thoughts that define what we resolve to do: our purpose, goals, and aims. Intentions direct us with determination toward action.

Think of the accomplishments in your life. They were the result of the fierce focus of all your energy toward a specific goal. You wanted to get a degree, buy a house, lose some weight, develop a career, or find a partner, and all of your actions were motivated by that intention.

One of the synonyms for the word intention is *design.* How perfect for a textile art! Knitting provides us with an opportunity to have designs on our designs. We may dedicate focused intention into each stitch of our project.

I'm reminded of a story of a devoutly Jewish knitter named Miriam who was making a special sweater for her sister to wear to an important job interview. It was Friday afternoon, and she still had two sleeves to knit. The interview was scheduled for the coming Monday, and Miriam was in a dilemma. Although she knew it was a mitzvah (good deed) to make this garment, how could she break Jewish law by knitting on the Sabbath? She came up with an innovative solution by making each stitch a thankful prayer to God for giving her the opportunity to support her sister. The sweater was finished on Monday, and Miriam's sister did indeed get that job.

ʬ

Why not cast good intentions into our knitting? In addition to being useful and beautiful, the fiber will be rich with our thoughts and dreams. There's a legacy of tying knots to cast spells. Marriage, of course, is the tying of a knot—binding the couple together. The veil that a bride wears began as a net protecting her from the evil eye. And in Greece, it was believed that tying a knot on an injured body part would stop blood flow. We know that now as a tourniquet, but at that time it was held to have magical powers.

What is a spell but an intention for a desired outcome? We can make each stitch an intention or a prayer that may be said out loud or quietly to ourselves. It might be something that we wish for ourselves, or it may be for someone else's healing. We can even project a global intention for world peace and understanding.

We may begin knitting with a particular intention or affirmation or let it emerge and transform as we work. Different intentions may appear on different days, depending upon what's happening at the time. Sometimes I begin knitting with a blank mind, and the appropriate affirmation will emerge. Often, my intention will simply mirror the process of making continuous interconnected knots. When gently anchoring each stitch, I'll find myself repeating: *I am secure. I am secure. I have a strong connection to myself and other people.*

I saw a *Nova* episode on PBS about mirror neurons in the brain. These neurons reflect whatever experience we're witnessing at the time and create empathy. For example, people get a vicarious thrill from watching sports, or they may cry at sad movies. Their brain activity mirrors that of the athlete or actor. I understand that these neurons reflect human interaction, but I wonder if they may also reflect the action of inanimate objects as well. What if our mirror neurons emulate the integration of the knots of knitting? We witness the fabric being knit together, and we, too, feel more whole.

Intention and Tension

Our hands make knitting a unique form of meditation. The constant and repetitive motion aids the flow of contemplation. Our hands hold the mantra. In fact, one of the first things we must do in knitting is to find the "gauge" or tension. How are we holding our knitting? Is it tight or loose? If we're wound tight, our knitting will be, too.

As you knit, you may see a record of your state of mind as you observe the tension in the fabric. I still get a chuckle when I look at a colorful scarf that I made while I was in the process of moving. There are brightly colored stripes with well-formed stitches in the beginning. As the scarf progressed and my packing became more stressful, tightly bunched patches of muddy colors appeared. By the time I was unpacking in my new home, the stitches loosened up and the colors evolved into pastel hues. The subtext of my story is revealed in the textile.

Our hands reveal the truth about our inner beliefs and motivations. They bear witness through the tautness of the fabric. Do we clutch our needles and pull our yarn, making it almost impossible to get the right-hand needle into the loop on the left-hand needle? If so, perhaps we may want to investigate our beliefs around control. Do we feel that we must worry, and watch everything and everybody? Do we believe that the world will fall apart if we aren't careful? Or do we feel as if we can't breathe because we're being strangled by our perfectionism or our ambition?

Our hands and knitting will reflect this tightness. Fiber, like us, needs room to breathe. Every stitch has a hole in the center. Tightly knit fabric won't lie flat because there's too little space in its center, and each stitch crowds the others. The fabric bunches and pulls from the stress, just as when our muscles get tense and filled with knots. Can we bring good intention to our lives (or knitting) if we're living (or knitting) with so much tension? What can we do?

It may not help to just say "Relax" to someone who's knitting tightly. I don't know about you, but I get more tense when someone tells me to relax! What we need is support and *focus* . . . and different tools. If you knit tightly, try using larger needles, which will create a looser tension. And don't try so hard. Trying too hard becomes *trying* after a while.

Often, we just need to lower our expectations in order to relax and have fun. Think of all those times in your life when you weren't invested in something working out perfectly, and it turned out surprisingly well. As an actor, I went to many auditions. It was often the times when I wasn't expecting or even caring if I got the part that I landed the job. Why? I had fun and was fully focused. It's the same in knitting and in life: Let yourself be in charge by giving up control of the outcome. Give yourself slack instead of flack.

Focus

Knitting too loosely can also provide clues about your inner intentions. If your project is floppy with lots of holes created from slipped stitches, it may indicate a lack of focus. Dropped stitches are dropped intentions, and too many indicate that your mind wanders. Do you go through life in a vague haze? Do you have a lot of unfinished objects (knitters commonly refer to them as "UFOs")? Do you have to redo projects because you first completed them in a haphazard manner? Do you forget things and find yourself easily distracted?

Your mind's meanderings may be trying to tell you something. But before you seek to "fix" the problem, look for a pattern in your fragmented thinking. Observe your thoughts without getting caught up in their tangled web. What purpose do they serve? Is there a hidden theme to all of the seemingly rambling musings? If you jump from thinking, *I have to pick up more vegetables for dinner* to *I wish that I could go to France* to *I hope I can fall asleep tonight,* you might notice a theme about needing nurturance. If you really listen to yourself, what do you hear?

Perhaps your flitting thoughts are trying to distract you from a deeper concern that you may want to avoid. Is your mind sending out decoys that are meant to sidetrack you on some minor crisis when there's a more important issue "underground"? It's easier to think about a broken vase than a marriage that's cracking apart. Sometimes it's helpful to ask yourself directly: *What would I like to avoid thinking about?* Although it's difficult to confront the truth, in the end it's more painful to avoid it. Going under the surgeon's knife may produce intense, short-lived pain that's preferable to the dull ache of a chronic, untreated illness. I invite you to use knitting as a practice for paying attention to what's in your hands and on your mind.

For more precise knitting, you may want to use a smaller-size needle and focus on one stitch at a time; you may clear your mind by zeroing in on specific thoughts one at a time. If you're noticing lots of dropped stitches and mind ramblings, this may be a time to give extra care and attention to the details of your life. Watch your thought patterns for clues about what may be bothering you on an unconscious level.

Try to have as much curiosity and compassion about your own mind and its wanderings as you would about a dear friend. Sometimes when my clients are lost or confused, I suggest that they see their situation like a film in their minds. They imagine that their lives are being portrayed by famous actors. While watching their life's "movie," I ask them what advice they wish they could offer the actor who's playing them. Often, they know exactly what they wish the protagonist would do or think. Imagining our lives as a movie is a great tool for developing objectivity. This exercise enables us to identify what's truly important to us so that we may take positive action when we're perplexed by difficult decisions.

The Whole World in Your Hands

Since yarn represents the thread of life, you're literally holding your symbolic life in your hands while knitting. You have the opportunity to make something useful and beautiful. As a knitter, you may develop great respect and love for your hands. I deeply appreciate the deftness and dependability of these parts of my body, which create lovely knitted garments and feel the texture of the fiber. My hands help me touch the world around me. Surgeons are encouraged to take up knitting to develop precision and manual dexterity. Hands have great memory as well. If you're returning to knitting after a long hiatus, you'll be amazed at how much your hands remember.

In addition to hand grooming so that your nails or cuticles don't snag the yarn, and using lotion to keep your skin soft, you can find other ways to appreciate your hands. Periodically while you knit, look lovingly at your hands and thank them. It may be fun to write a poem or song to honor your hands, wrists, arms, and fingers as well.

Counting Meditation

Another method of knitting meditation is counting stitches. You may do this silently or aloud, and the focus of counting will serve as a mantra to clear your mind. As is the case with any meditation, if random thoughts and mental chatter appear, just witness them without attachment and let them go. Then return to the counting. This method is useful, as it also keeps you honest about dropping or adding stitches.

Eyes-Shut, Mind-Open Meditation

For those of you who are experienced knitters, or for those confident souls who want to take on a challenge, try knitting a simple stitch pattern with your eyes closed. You can do it! In *Elizabeth Zimmermann's Knitter's Almanac,* this wise guru of sensible knitting, said: "What? You can't knit in the dark? Stuff and nonsense; anybody can. Shut your eyes. Knit one stitch. Open your eyes and look at the stitch; it's all right. Shut your eyes and knit two stitches."

I know many prolific knitters who are visually challenged. Knitting develops our tactile sense. After having contact with a wide variety of yarns, we touch everything with more feeling and sensitivity. I'm always amazed at how knowledgeable my hands are when I'm in the dark and need to find my way.

Merely closing your eyes produces relaxing alpha waves in your brain. Knitting with your eyes closed can produce a deep meditative state because you also get the benefit of the steady repetition of your hands, which serves as a rhythmic, tactile mantra. Your mind can be free of specific thoughts; or you may repeat any favorite prayer, chant, intention, or affirmation. As in any meditation practice, it's important to witness any chatter or stray thoughts as you try to keep the focus on your hands, as well as on your regular breath.

Knitting a Better World

One of the most vital and profound experiences in life is helping others, and all the major religions hold charity as an important virtue. In Hebrew school, we'd collect money in a little box for good causes. The container was called the *tzedakah* box. As an adult, I've learned that the Hebrew word *tzedakah* doesn't translate as "charity." It means "justice." It's not enough to offer assistance merely because it's a nice thing to do; it's the necessary way we heal the planet. Knitting for someone who needs help is a meaningful experience that provides the recipient with the warmth of a hat, sweater, pair of gloves, and human kindness. It reminds the knitters that they're compassionate members of the human family. Everyone benefits.

Sue Manning, who created the Knitting Connection, an organization dedicated to supporting children and families with crafted items utilizing the artistic talents of volunteer knitters, says, "No child should be without a hat or mittens. We connect people to support each other during their time of need. This link forms a bond of understanding and love." Find out more about the Knitting Connection by visiting their Website: **www.theknittingconnection.org**.

The Shawl Ministry is a grassroots effort begun by Janet Bristow and Victoria Galo, who combined their love of knitting with their spiritual faith and desire to help others. They established a ministry to create and give away prayer shawls to those in need or experiencing a life passage. "What we do is moved by 'Spirit,'" Victoria Galo says, "It is passed from hand-to-hand and heart-to-heart. It's that humble and simple." Shawl Ministry groups are everywhere. You may check their Website at **www.shawlministry.com** to learn more.

There are numerous organizations that provide knitting for charity. You can start your own or simply knit for someone you know who may need the comfort that hand knitting provides. Knitting for others is an important way to make a contribution. The inner and outer rewards are infinite: Think globally, knit locally!

It Helps You

The plane was delayed for over an hour, and the prospect of missing my connecting flight was becoming increasingly evident. I was anxious. I had an important appointment in Denver, and I couldn't miss it. I had no recourse but to pull out my knitting and vent my frustration into the yarn and needles. Throughout the wait, the woman sitting next to me watched as a brightly colored sock took shape. Finally, she smiled at me and said in a thick Russian accent: "Eet halps you."

She's right. Knitting calms my jangled nerves and soothes me when I'm feeling high-strung. If insomnia strikes, I know I can grasp my project and knit up the raveled sleeve of my cares to paraphrase Shakespeare. *It helps me.* Many people also feel that knitting is a form of therapy; the extraordinary writer Virginia Woolf said, "Knitting is the saving of life."

Knitting helps other people as well. I visited the Klarman Eating Disorders Center at Harvard-affiliated McLean Hospital where many of the young patients were knitting intently throughout the campus. Their expressive therapist told me that the girls, ages 13 to 23, have become zealous knitters over the past few years. They've been selling their scarves, hats, mittens, and socks to raise money for various charities.

Knitting provides them with a calm, steadfast focus that assists them in their recovery. An eating disorder indicates that a person feels empty inside and is looking for a way to fill the void—and knitting can help satisfy the hunger to be whole. Sometimes, the insatiable need for food that accompanies an eating disorder is transferred onto the craft, and the girls knit incessantly. The therapists agree that it's much better for the girls to be constantly knitting rather than starving themselves or bingeing and purging. As the therapists help the girls identify the source of their emptiness, the young women are able to receive the nourishment that knitting offers: peace of mind, generosity, community, and a sense of accomplishment.

Knitting is also being used as a tool for prisoner rehabilitation. Many correctional facilities across the United States are discovering that instituting programs of knitting and crocheting helps inmates develop patience, anger management, and social skills. Using donated yarn and strictly monitored plastic tools, the inmates are making scarves, blankets, and toys for charities.

Many of the men and women in prison have never learned a skill. The sense of accomplishment that they experience by making something unique from their own hands, time, and imagination gives them an enormous boost of self-confidence. They feel more respect for themselves and others as a result. Knitting repairs the torn fibers in their lives . . . *it helps them.*

chapter 20

Tinking, Frogging, Toads, and Princes

"Anyone who has never made a mistake has never tried anything new."

— Albert Einstein

A re you ready for the real truth about knitting? Every knitter now and forever knows this indisputable fact: "As you knit, so shall you rip."

Ripping out is an inevitable and commonplace part of the craft. Are you starting to break out in a cold sweat? Is your perfectionism saying, *Oh no! Make mistakes! Admit I made them! Rip out my work? I'd rather put the knitting needles in my eyes! Oh, horror, horror!* If you're hearing these inner voices, then knitting will be a great life teacher for you. And don't worry—you're in good company. There are scores of people around the globe right now scowling at the knitting in their laps and wondering how 12 extra stitches appeared or disappeared, and how the heck that hole emerged and when.

We're human beings and prone to mistakes. I think we forget that little piece of information sometimes. As Daena mentioned, the goddess Athena's obsession with making the most perfect weaving drove her to turn the mortal Arachne into a spider. Perfection is not a pretty picture. The Native Americans will intentionally weave in mistakes so as not to offend the goddess Spider Woman. I may never get to the point where I have to *intentionally* knit mistakes, so the gods can rest easy with me. The point is that we aren't invincible— we're human.

Blemishes may even be interesting or useful. In his book *The Empty Space,* Peter Brook wrote that when they were developing synthetic music, the Austrians discovered that to replicate the sound of any instrument, they had to add noise—shuffles, coughs, and scrapes. Imperfection gave the tone authenticity. Similarly, the yarns I love most are those that have remnants of the sheep's journey through brambles, the irregular thick and thin of the spinner's hand, and all the colors that come from the earth. You're making something with your hands, so it needn't look as if it came from a machine. It's *handmade.*

Mistakes are badges of our humanity. What might happen if you change your intention from achieving perfection to simply enjoying an activity? I believe that full absorption in the process of any task brings quality to the product's outcome. Are you giving care and attention to each stitch? Do you love it? If so, it will be lovely.

What are mistakes? How do they happen? Let's examine the word *mistake:* It's a missed taking. When making a film, each try is called a "take." The "keeper" is the take that's alive with all the desired emotional and artistic elements. We must be awake to get a good take.

Mistakes are monuments to moments when you weren't present, moments you missed taking. You forgot to call the airlines or your mother-in-law. You didn't tell your daughter that she did a splendid job on her homework, or perhaps you dropped ice cream on the sidewalk. Are you bad for that? No. Your mind was buzzing with other missions. Maybe you were trying desperately to solve a problem, or perhaps you were engaged in the 21st century's favorite sport of multitasking. The old Buddhist aphorism rings true here: *Chop wood. Carry water.* When you chop wood, really chop the wood. When you carry water, just carry the water. You're focused and present.

Tinkering with Our Coat of Armor

I've learned the hard way that I must pay attention when I knit. I was in the middle of moving out of state to a great house and also making a turtleneck pullover with some colorful variegated wool. I was almost finished and working on the neck, when I held the sweater up to myself and realized that the opening was absurdly small. How did that happen? Wanting to be finished with the project, I desperately examined the neck from all angles. It *must* be the right size—I was following a pattern. It must be okay . . . but it was *not* okay. No matter how I looked at it, I saw my future: I must rip.

As I ripped out two weeks' worth of work, something dawned on me: I was slowly taking out each stitch with the eye of a detective looking for clues. I wanted to find the origin of the mistake. Where did I go astray? It occurred to me that this process was similar to that of psychotherapy. In therapy, I need to probe my mind and unravel the messages I learned about life in order to understand which ones are true and which are false. Therapy can be a slow and methodical process, just like ripping out my turtleneck.

I eventually discovered the root of the error: I was off one stitch each row. All it took was one extra decreased stitch repeated every few rows to make a huge mistake. All it takes is one lie repeated in your head for many moments, many years, to create a defensive behavior to deal with the hurt of that toxic message.

If children are repeatedly told they are stupid, ugly, or selfish, you know what happens. They believe it. If we buy into a lie, we feel hurt and need to defend against the pain. Defenses are behaviors that protect us, but they're also offensive and push people away. If children aren't taken seriously, they learn to space out and avoid responsibility. If they bear the brunt of massive criticism, they may develop a steely hard and cold manner, or they may react to the criticism by acting weak or passive.

When children are painfully withdrawn and shy after years of being told that they aren't good enough, it's understandable. They're doing the best they can, given all those hurtful messages. Our defenses may have protected us long ago, but they don't serve us now. They're cumbersome coats of armor that were custom-made according to the lies that tailored them.

Lies are only powerful if you believe them. If I tell you that you're a purple Martian, you'll either laugh or think I'm insane. You know that you're not a Martian and aren't purple—this information doesn't push on any emotional buttons. So if you uncover the hurtful messages that you *do* believe in (such as not being good enough, smart enough, or "whatever" enough) and discover that they are indeed lies and *not* reality, the truth will set you free.

Using knitting as a metaphor, can we imagine ripping out our defenses? Maybe we can unravel them slowly, with care. With the spirit of the sleuth, we can take out the stitches of false beliefs that hinder us and eventually reknit our life the way we want it. Many of us are filled with blame and shame for our defensive behaviors and thoughts. If we understand the origins of our defenses, we may have more compassion for ourselves and see that our defensive behavior isn't our fault. Given all the false messages and circumstances of our lives, we came by every defense honestly. What could we have done differently? When we aren't bound up by blame, we may take the responsibility to dismantle the faulty fabric of the past and truly change.

Mistakes may be flashlights that illuminate our subconscious thoughts. Was it a coincidence that I made my turtleneck chokingly small when I was trying to expand my circumstances by moving to a bigger and better home? Perhaps the slipup was a subconscious expression of my fear that I was "getting a big head," or maybe it was acting out the lie that I don't deserve a nicer home. If we see missteps as messengers of our subconscious beliefs, we may find that our "errors" are dynamic tools for self-dialogue and growth. Nothing gets our attention in life—or in knitting—like a big mistake! We learn from mistakes.

By the way, there's a name for the careful stitch-by-stitch method I used when taking out the variegated turtleneck. We say that we're going to "tink," which is "knit" spelled backward. The process of self-growth requires us to go back and *tink*er with our broken-down belief systems and replace them with a new and improved truth.

Messages from Mistakes

Some years ago, I was knitting myself a coat that described the time my ten-year marriage ripped apart. I was euphoric with my newfound freedom, so I knit two tap dancers who sported hats and canes. It was a complicated pattern (as was my marriage) with many colors and repetitions. When I was finished with the dancers, I noticed that they both had one extra stitch on their feet. It looked as if they had clubfeet.

The prospect of ripping out a large section of fuzzy, entangling mohair seemed daunting, and I left the "error" in. But on closer inspection, I realized that those feet were no mistake—in fact, this was the true picture of my life at the time. I was just learning how to "dance" in my new single life, and truthfully, I was a little clumsy. I was dancing in spite of my metaphorical clubfeet.

A blunder can also be an opportunity for discovery. The correcting fluid Liquid Paper was invented because of a typist who used white paint to cover her errors. The recipe for chocolate chip cookies was created when the owner of the Toll House Inn ran out of powdered baker's chocolate and substituted semisweet bits of chocolate.

I heard a story about a girl named Esche in a fourth-grade knitting class who made a "mistake" when she was knitting with three colors. Instead of carrying her yarn in the back, she dragged it to the front, and created a crownlike effect. She thought it looked cool and asked her teacher if she could leave it in. The rest of the class integrated her technique into their hats, and they called this effect an "Esche." Sometimes a mistake is not a mistake.

MM

Knitting can definitely bring passion to the surface. This is illustrated in the story of the "Sweater Slasher." Janet and Don, a couple who owns a terrific yarn store called Putting On the Knitz, told me that one day a sweet, mild-mannered woman came into the store to buy yarn. She was going to make a sweater for her teenage granddaughter. The woman spent many hours deciding upon the pattern and yarn, and finally settled on a simple design that used very expensive wool.

A few months later, she returned and announced that her granddaughter's sweater was wrong and she must buy more yarn. Janet and Don suggested that she rip out the cardigan and reuse the yarn since it was so lovely and costly, but the grandmother said she couldn't do that. She told Don that when she discovered that the sleeves were off-kilter, she was so upset that she took out a sharp butcher knife and slashed it. Perhaps she played the soundtrack music from Hitchcock's film *Psycho* as she did her deadly deed—Charles Dickens's character Madame Defarge and her stitches of vengeance had nothing on the Sweater Slasher!

Don told me that according to his knowledge of that pattern and the woman's description of how it looked, he was certain that the sweater was indeed *correct!* I wonder if the moral of the story is to wait a few hours before ripping— or slashing—your work. But then again, maybe her sweater slashing provided a primal emotional release for her. Therapy comes in many forms.

Frogging

There are times when you must come to terms with a serious error. This is no longer a boo-boo; it's a disaster. You hate the design, color, and pattern. It's totally wrong, and the mistake is beyond Band-Aids. These are times for "frogging." When you know a large section has to be reworked and you must do some serious ripping, you can take the needles out and pull on the yarn so that all the stitches come undone quickly.

Why do knitters call it frogging? Well, when you unravel the yarn quickly, you "rip it, rip it, rip it" like the sound of a frog. Most knitters will tell you that after the initial moments of regret, remorse, and rage, there's redemption. Free at last! You don't have to live with that horrible mistake.

Do you want to know an interesting coincidence? Frogs are the Mayan symbols of purification! So by frogging, you're cleansing yourself of that which you don't want. You may begin anew.

I think the horror that some people experience when frogging (or witnessing it) is fear of impermanence. How can someone *intentionally* destroy something that took that much time and effort to make? It seems like creativity homicide. I'm reminded of those gorgeous and highly intricate mandala sandpaintings that are destroyed by the monks who made them. They poured time, concentration, and effort into that image. How can they sweep it away? The monks say that they're inspired to make the mandala purely for the *energy* that's released in the moment of creation. When they're finished, the experience is over and they destroy the mandala. Soon they'll create another.

In my early knitting years, I was indignant at the idea of ripping out: *Are you kidding? I have to begin again after all that time and effort? How dare the knitting do this to me? How dare I make a mistake?* The recriminations and condemnations started to flow. If your intention is to enjoy the process, what difference does it make if you knit ten inches again? If you love to knit, just knit.

I remember taking a hike on a scenic desert trail and getting angry with myself for forgetting something back at my tent. As I retraced my steps back to the campground, I started to look around and noticed how beautiful the path was from the opposite perspective. My intention was to walk in the splendor of nature, so what difference did it make if I was coming or going?

Can you "do a row over" in life? Often you can. Let's say that you spoke harshly and regret it. You might apologize. Or maybe you withheld your truth and compromised your integrity in a meeting. You can contact the group and speak your mind honestly. Did you break a promise to yourself or another? Go back and fulfill your word. Do you have regrets about not learning a skill? Join a class. Take a risk if you played it safe.

It's terrible to be stuck with mistakes that will haunt you for the rest of your life—but you don't have to live with them. Ripping out is a knitter's prerogative and privilege. Rid yourself of what you don't want, reknit, and enjoy the results. As you gain experience and expertise, eliminating unwanted errors may be a way of developing higher standards of excellence. In my own life, I notice that I find myself surrounded by friends of greater depth and substance as I grow.

Ripping out gives us a good perspective on life. After unraveling many weeks' worth of knitting and living to tell the tale, we develop the invaluable attitude of taking things in stride. Life may be precious, but we don't need to be precious about life (or knitting, for that matter).

〰

We were in a knitting group when Julia discovered that she'd made the entire front of her sweater so large that even the Jolly Green Giant would find it too big. It was huge! As she ripped out, she started to giggle. Pretty soon, Julia was laughing uncontrollably while she frogged this disaster . . . and her laughter was contagious. Every unraveled row seemed hilarious.

Julia was unraveling more than a sweater: She was ripping out the absurdity of life that we all experience from time to time. Tears streamed down my face, and my stomach hurt from laughing. Our group bonded through the laughter.

The next week, Julia returned with an important insight about that sweater. She realized that it mirrored her distorted

perception of her body image. While knitting, she kept thinking, *This is going to be way too small for me. I need to make
it bigger.* Julia is a beautiful, big-boned woman, perhaps a
size 14, but certainly not as huge as the 50-inch front of her
sweater. She said that laughing while frogging the sweater
expressed her great relief in ridding herself of that hurtful and
untruthful self-perception.

Toads and Princes

There are times when we aren't ready to frog, and that's
when "Toad" appears—"Trashed Object Abandoned in Dis-
gust." Toads are all of those unfinished projects stashed in
bags and shoved into closets, drawers, or attics. How many
times in our lives have we shelved something that we knew in
our hearts was wrong but couldn't release? When we're ready
to face the reality of "I don't want this thing, person, place,
occupation in my life anymore—I can let go," then we're able
to do the demolition of frogging. Toads create clutter that
gather dust and guilt.

Just as in the stories of old, if we kiss the frog or toad and
truly dare to love ourselves, warts and all, we may turn a Toad
into a "Prince," a "Project Resurrected into a New Creative
Endeavor." A Prince is another chance, a fresh start. Frog a
Toad to find a Prince, and you may begin the marvelous journey again. As you knit, so shall you rip.

chapter 21

Tangling Conversation

*"I say that I am myself, but what is this self
of mine but a knot in the tangled skein of
things where chance and change combine?"*
— Don Marquis

Tangles are a unique cauldron of transformation. May she
who has a life that's tangle free throw the first skein. I think
snarls in knitting and in life are both unavoidable and prevent-
able. And if the paradox of that thought just gave your mind
a twist, welcome to the world of tangles!

Nature is filled with these complicated twists, such as
vines, ivy, and even black holes in space. Scientists postulate
that each black hole is crammed with matter, like a giant,
fuzzy, tangled knot held together forever by gravity. I read an
article posted at the Fisher Center for Alzheimer's Research
Foundation's Website **(alzinfo.org)**, stating that Alzheimer's disease may develop because of "potentially damaging
tangles formed by a protein called 'tau.' Normally, tau forms
structures in the brain that help provide nourishment to brain

cells. But in Alzheimer's disease, the tau protein forms thread-like deposits within brain cells, called neurofibrillary tangles."

Tangles are the *discord* in life. They're metaphors for problems that need to be solved. Can we do anything constructive to deal with snarls and knots in our yarn? How do we prevent them in our lives? In knitting, I find that tangles occur for four reasons:

1. We're not paying attention.
2. We're multitasking beyond our capabilities.
3. We don't separate the yarn and give it enough space.
4. We inherit the tangle from an outside source.

Many tangles occur if we're not paying attention. Put two strands of anything down, anyplace, add a breeze or some movement, and if we're distracted . . . voilà, la tangle! We must forgive ourselves for getting into snarls with our yarn, as well as with the fibers of our lives.

Okay, so you're knitting with two strands of color when you look at the clock and realize with a start that you have to get to the dentist for your dreaded root canal. You stuff your knitting into your bag, knowing that he's always late. You think, *I may have an opportunity to knit.* In the waiting room, you discover that your yarn is mingled with your cell phone's "hands-free" ear wire and caught in the snap of your change purse. Your knitting has become a naughty, knotty mess. It happens to the best of us.

Here are a few tips to save you from tangle trauma: If you're working with more than one color, try cutting small, manageable strands instead of using the entire balls of yarn, which will inevitably intertwine and make trouble. You can separate the colors by putting them into little plastic sandwich bags. There are actually accessories on the market called "yarn bras" that separate and support each ball of yarn in order to prevent tangles.

Perhaps we might apply this to our lives: Do we give ourselves enough time and space? I'm often impressed at how much I can accomplish when I return from vacation, or even just a few unscheduled hours. Rushing around and cramming chores and activities into the day often creates a snarl of stress and many mistakes.

Clutter also creates tangles. How can we find any order in our minds if we can't find anything on our desk? When my office becomes littered with yellow sticky notes that quote Thoreau's admonition, "Simplify, simplify," I know that it's time to clean out my drawers and give myself more space. Decluttering is one of the best tangle remedies I know.

Anticipation aids in tangle prevention as well. If we foresee that going to the doctor or visiting disapproving relatives may make us feel tense and out of control, we might prevent potential tangles if we give ourselves extra kindness and some preparation. Get information about anything that may be provocative. Develop secret signals with your significant other to indicate that it's time to leave when Uncle Harold has had a few too many martinis. We can't guarantee that the situation will be knot free, but it may be more manageable, with fewer kinks.

We may also inherit a tangle. Sometimes the skein, ball, or hank of yarn comes from the mill or spinning wheel with unseen knots. We're innocently knitting away when a snarled mess appears, blocking the next stitch. In life, we may be born into a multitude of tangles and emotional snags that are passed down from generation to generation.

Many people yank on the yarn when encountering a tangle. Repeated tugging creates more tightness and is rarely a solution. There's a technique to untangling. We can't undo a snarl all at once. Tangles respond well when we pull them apart to find the slack thread and methodically trace the course of this strand to a knot, which we must patiently undo. We proceed in this manner, knot to knot, winding up whatever slack we can create until the matted mass is undone.

In life, we often have reflexive reactions to situations that cause us to yank on the various strands of our lives. Do we snap at our mate, child, friend, or relative every time they say something that frustrates us? Does our impatience ever *really* get us what we want? If we feel tugged upon, we tighten up and make a tangled situation more difficult. The complication is an opportunity to experiment with new behaviors and responses.

What happens if we listen to our child's reasons for failing a class instead of scolding? What if we look for humor and laugh (or knit!) when caught in a traffic jam? How about breathing and disengaging from a conflict with our client when we're most upset? If we feel that we're caught in an overwhelmingly problematic situation, perhaps we may follow the same technique that we do for detangling yarn.

We may not be able to solve the whole difficulty at once. But if we proceed from issue to issue, giving ourselves slack and finding solutions for each small conflict we encounter, eventually our tenacity and attention will enable us to find a resolution for the overriding problem.

Labyrinths and Mazes

Tangled yarn (in most cases) is just one unbroken strand of fiber. It's reassuring to know that with time, concentration, and effort, the knotted twists will eventually be disentangled. I'm reminded of labyrinths and mazes. A labyrinth is a circuitous course with one way in and one way out that has come to symbolize the path of life. A maze is a puzzle filled with dead ends and cul-de-sacs.

A journey through a labyrinth may be a meditation to help answer questions and quiet the mind. Tangles may be meditations, also, but we too often associate judgment and blame with them: The stupid yarn company wound the hank wrong; the dog, child, or cat did it. Usually, we get angry with ourselves: We were careless; we were dumb. We can be relentless when it comes to blame, but if we remove the condemnation, what remains is a puzzle that must be solved.

There's a difference between blaming ourselves for a tangled situation and taking responsibility for untangling it. When we think that things are our fault, we may feel weak and resistant to change. But if we see our contribution to a problem without blaming ourselves, we feel strong and we can take responsibility in order to make a difference.

If we leave the window open and rain saturates our roommate's CD player, we have two choices: We can berate ourselves and avoid talking to him or her, or we can take responsibility by admitting that we made a thoughtless mistake. The second choice gives us the confidence to offer a sincere apology and make amends.

A tangle in life may also be telling us that our minds are filled with "nots," negative thoughts of what we lack, instead of gratitude for the bounty in our life. In her book *I Can Do It*, Louise Hay says, "Dwelling on lack only creates more lack. Poverty thinking brings more poverty. Gratitude thinking brings abundance."

Having allies is always helpful when confronting life's tangles. According to the myth, when Theseus entered the labyrinth to slay the dangerous Minotaur, he was given a ball of yarn by Ariadne to help him find his way out. What a kind and resourceful woman! Ariadne knew that following our true fiber is a lifesaver when we enter the labyrinth to slay our inner demons.

You learn a lot about a person by their relationship to tangles. I have a friend who's a "tangle trooper." Lucy often observes me fighting with a ragged clump of fiber resembling roadkill and quietly asks, "May I help?" She diligently and lovingly disengages the yarn without any trace of recrimination or condescension.

I'm taken not only with her untangling facility and patience, but also her enormous kindness and generosity. A friend when you're in tangle need is a friend indeed. Perhaps for Lucy, the snarl is merely fun—a challenging puzzle, a maze of knots. She has no blame or shame attached to it, no condemnation. What if we could regard the tangles in our personal life in that way?

Knitters learn to know when to undo tangles and when to cut them. This lesson applies to life. Sometimes we need to have the incisiveness of Alexander the Great who cut the challenging Gordian knot. We need to know when to work on a relationship and when to leave.

We have to tell the difference between being in a labyrinth or a maze. If we're lost in a maze of confusion and feel as if our life situation is at a dead end, then it might be a good idea to call for help. When our knitting starts to resemble matted dreadlocks, sometimes cutting is the only solution. Snip away what's terribly knotted, sacrifice the yarn, and move on.

We do that in life when a relationship has gone beyond repair. It's a sign of strength, actually, to know when the emotional tangle is past hope, and it's time to leave a relationship that's no longer working. Tangles can be great guides that help us develop insight, flexibility, patience, character, humor, and—most important—compassion as we journey in the labyrinth of life.

TANGLE

chapter 22

Knitting Patterns
for Life

"To see things in the seed, that is genius."
— Lao Tzu

N ow that we've looked at the creative process through the life metaphors of knitting, it's time to knit! I've designed two projects that will give you a contemplative experience with this art form. The first pattern is perfect for beginners or experienced knitters who'd like to use knitting as a meditation. You'll find pattern instructions and information about where to purchase the yarn at the end the book. I recommend that you read this chapter before you begin the project.

Seeds of Intention Scarf

This scarf is all about softness and solitude. It's about finding a corner in your house and a time in your day to be reflective and self-loving. It's about knitting seeds of positive intentions, affirmations, wishes, hopes, prayers, and gratitude into every stitch. If you're going to do the difficult, sometimes

SEEDS OF INTENTION SCARF VERSION 1

SEEDS OF INTENTION SCARF VERSION 2

SEEDS OF INTENTION SCARF VERSION 3 MOBIUS

gritty, work of self-growth, then you deserve a lot of softness. Sometimes the world can be a hard place. Navigating our life is challenging enough without all the unexpected obstacles that cross our path or the emotional boils that get pressed from time to time.

The yarn I've chosen for this scarf is white and fluffy, like a light-filled cloud. White light is symbolic of hope, truth, and grace. No matter where we live in the world, light from the sun is something we all have in common; we share the same sky. This yarn also reminds me of cotton balls. When I'm having a difficult time, Daena will often tell me that she wants to wrap me in a million cotton balls, and her kind intention always makes me feel better.

Let the knitting of this scarf be a sacred and intimate ritual. This isn't a transportable project that's meant for the hustle and bustle of the world. Designate a special corner or room that will be a private place for your knitting. Light a white candle, burn some sage to cleanse the air, and play your favorite soothing music. Wash your hands and put a white cloth on your lap to keep the yarn's color pure; place the yarn and needles in a favorite bag or basket.

Bring a meaningful object into the space to create an altar when you knit—try planting an actual seed of a favorite flower, fruit, or vegetable in a little pot of dirt in this area. Treat the yarn and needles with the care you'd want for yourself. Imagine that when you touch the fiber, you're holding your dreams and hopes for a better world. Let this knitting deepen your self-love and respect. Take your time. It's not a project to hurry through and finish; it's something to savor. Even knitting five rows or spending five minutes will be a special part of your daily meditation.

Using Affirmations

Find personal affirmations of kindness and hopes for peace while creating this scarf. Here are some possibilities: *I feel peace around me and within me. I am healthy and whole. I find insight and delight. I am strong and sturdy.* Sow the seeds of those beliefs into the scarf itself, and you and your project will grow together. Each stitch is a seed that you plant with intention; each one affirms: *Yes, I am knitting myself together in a loving way.*

You can change your outer circumstances by transforming your negative thoughts into positive beliefs. Affirmations will work best if you truly *believe* them. However, it's not always easy to go from negative to positive thinking. The roots of negativity are usually attached to deep pain and hurt that was created in the past, and it can be difficult to let go of your old programming. Self-destructive thinking is formed by relentless repetition; and the good news is that conscious positive repetition of compassionate affirmations can undo the damage. Change *is* possible. If you drip water continuously on a rock, an indentation will form. There will be an impact.

When we understand what determinants caused our self-destructive thoughts, we may have more compassion for ourselves. Cleaning out the old wounds enables us to develop more self-love, which then helps us commit to the affirmative, healthy thinking that will change the very fabric of our belief systems and enable us to attract more love, wealth, inspiration, joy, health, and abundance. We deserve to enjoy life.

The Dawn of Optimism

I was helping Dawn work on a sweater design for her two-year-old daughter, Shayna. Dawn wanted to put symbols on the sweater that represented the delight that the little girl brought to the family. I suggested a hummingbird since they represent joy, so we found a needlework graph of the beautiful bird. Dawn looked at it for a moment and then shook her head, saying, "No, I can't do that. It won't turn out well. It's too complicated." I searched my books and found another hummingbird, this one simple and elegant. Dawn looked leery and said that she imagined that the blue, lavender, and green colors she'd chosen were probably wrong for it.

While we were casting on, she told me offhandedly that she hadn't been able to spend much time on this sweater because she was looking for employment. She'd been laid off from her administrative-assistant job about a year ago and had been sending out massive amounts of résumés with what she described as "futile results."

I wondered if there was a connection between the negative predicting she did with her sweater and her "futile" job hunt. I asked Dawn where she got the idea that nothing works out well and all her efforts would be rejected. She said she wasn't sure. Eventually, she talked about her large family in which she was the youngest child and the only daughter in a group of five sons.

Her brothers had teased and taunted her daily about being a loser. They said she was useless and couldn't do anything right. Her mother was a nice woman, but felt helpless to intervene since she was already overwhelmed by trying to hold the family together while her husband was sick with Hodgkin's disease. Dawn felt doomed as a child. She knew that her father was going to die, and she couldn't do anything about it. She felt that failure was her most constant companion in life.

In spite of this, Dawn never considered herself a negative person. As she thought about her life, she became understandably upset and angry. How dare her brothers cast her in the role of "designated flunky" in the family? Why didn't her parents protect her and help her see the truth: that she was strong and capable? I said that having a good life was the best revenge. From this moment on, she didn't need to buy into the lies of being a loser, but instead could regard herself as a resilient woman who'd survived a challenging childhood.

I suggested that she make a Seeds of Intention Scarf in this period while she was looking for a new job. Dawn took time in the morning to sit in solitude and knit with beautiful white wool. She lit a candle and visualized specific details about her ideal job: the environment in which she'd work, her desk, the convenient location, the challenging assignments, her friendly co-workers, and a likable boss. While knitting, she said positive affirmations aloud that she was strong, capable, and deserving, and that the world can be a place of positive bounty and generosity.

Dawn did this for a week. She said that she felt calmer and happier, and she loved her personal knitting time. She started to look forward to calling prospective employers and having fruitful interviews. She had more fun mailing her résumés.

In the past, she'd dump them into the mailbox and think, *Here goes nothing. A bunch of rejections is all I'll get from this.* Now she noticed that she regarded the résumés as seeds and was excited to anticipate what kind of garden she might harvest from them.

A few weeks after she began her Seeds of Intention Scarf, Dawn was invited in for three interviews. She thoroughly enjoyed meeting with each interviewer, and two of the firms offered her a job. Dawn spent the next morning knitting her scarf with the intention of deciding which opportunity she should take. In the end, she chose the one that most closely resembled her visualization.

I saw Dawn recently and she was smiling. She loves her job and was working consciously on keeping her tendency to be pessimistic in check. She also showed me the hummingbird sweater she knitted for Shayna. I marveled at the details of the bird's wings and the shimmering enchantment of the lavender, blue, and green. The sweater was a tribute to delight itself.

The Symbolism of the Seeds of Intention Scarf

This scarf will warm and protect your throat, which is the seat of the fifth chakra energy point of the body. This is the center of breath, communication, and personal power. Your voice allows you to ask for what you want in the world; it's the way you speak your mind. Knitting affirmations of strength and self-love into your scarf will help you voice your truth with more conviction.

The stitch we use (knit, purl, and then in the next row, purl on a knit stitch, and knit on a purl stitch) is actually named the "Seed Stitch." Sometimes it's called "Moss Stitch" or "Rice Stitch." Seeds promote growth. Moss is soft. Rice nourishes. Think of your stitches as seeds for self-love, and relax on the soft mossy carpet of life's mysterious forest. Remember that gardens take time to grow. We need to fertilize and water ourselves with patience, kindness, and insight.

Numbers are significant to this scarf. Throughout the ages, numbers have been used to measure and understand the universe. It was written in the book of Solomon from the Old Testament (also known as the book of Wisdom): "Thou hast arranged all things by measure and number and weight."

Plato called the study of numerology the "highest level of knowledge" and Pythagoras said, "Numbers rule all things." Numbers have profound symbolic meaning in many mystical practices such as the Kabbalah, sacred geometry, I Ching, the tarot, and numerology.

The Seed Scarf is 17 stitches wide. Seventeen may be reduced to its essential number by adding: $1 + 7 = 8$. The number eight is highly symbolic. Because of its shape, it's considered to represent infinity; it also symbolizes transcendence and spirituality. In the book of Genesis, the world was created in six days, and the seventh day is marked for rest and contemplation of the earth's completion. The eighth day is beyond the making of the world. Christ was resurrected on the eighth day. The eighth note of the octave goes beyond the seven tones of a musical scale and begins a new scale.

The number eight invites us to reach beyond our limits while containing the earthly grounding of the number four. (Eight is comprised of two sets of four.) Four is associated with the material world: There are four seasons, four elements (earth, air, fire, and water), and four directions. The number eight represents our potential for expansion and growth.

ᘉ

While you're knitting, you may think of tangible ways to plant positive seeds of growth in your life. For instance, if you want to have more friends and community, you may consider sowing the seeds of friendship by visualizing yourself calling people to say hello or arranging to meet for lunch. If you'd like to develop your career, you may think of more places to send out résumés to "seed" your professional aspirations. If you long to feel more self-love, you may plant the seeds of self-care by considering getting some massage, counseling, or exercise.

When you're finished with your knitting session, you can actually put these thoughts into action. Call your friends, make self-care appointments, and send out résumés. The more seeds you plant, the greater the promise of an abundant harvest. When finished, your scarf is more than an accessory—it's an account of your time, your meditation, and affirmations. It's a fabric filled with seeds of love.

(Pattern and yarn information are at the end of this book in the section entitled "Knitting Patterns.")

The Cape of Constant Change

"Change alone is eternal, perpetual, immortal"
— Schopenhauer

This next design offers a few more challenges, but it's still easy. Have no fear: Just bring beginner's mind and enjoy every stitch. Remember, you can always rip it out and start over if you make a mistake! Once again, you'll find the pattern directions and information about where to purchase the yarn at the end of the book. I recommend that you read this chapter before you begin the project.

This cape is a celebration of change. I chose this extraordinary yarn that contains vibrant variations of red, purple, turquoise, green, and gold—not just because it's beautiful, but also because its fiber tells many stories of change. Being 100 percent silk, its threads have come from the silkworm, a creature of metamorphosis. The silkworm spins a cocoon the size of a peanut, and each cocoon is composed of a single strand that can stretch a mile long. The strands are woven to create the silk fabric that is used in saris, the traditional garments of southern Asian women.

CAPE OF CONSTANT CHANGE

Saris are shape-shifting garments: They're made of rectangular cloth that's draped to flatter the form of the body; when the wearer takes it off, it morphs back to its original rectangular shape. Here's my favorite part of the story: There are small, family-run cottage industries in Nepal that collect the remnant scraps of this colorful sari silk from the cutting-room floor and spin them into splendid yarn. They take what's *cast off* and make it possible for us to *cast on* a magnificent new garment. This is a tale of retrieving what was seemingly worthless and transforming it into something useful and valuable. The colors are brilliant, and the cloth is often rich with symbols. This sari silk is the same sacred cloth that's used for Tibetan peace flags and religious banners. Spirit is woven into the fabric.

Metamorphosis

A cape can be a cocoon or a chrysalis. We're wrapped in swaddling when we greet the world as infants, and this binding makes us feel secure. Similarly, capes wrap around us and remind us that we're safe. Safety is an essential element for us to change and grow. Remember that the silkworm needs the security of the cocoon to develop. Within the shell of protection, tremendous change is taking place. The caterpillar completely reconstitutes itself by growing and shedding its skin at least five or six times. Most of its life is spent inside the chrysalis, and very little time is actually spent as a moth or butterfly.

The silkworm's experience offers a metaphor for our personal growth. We, too, remake ourselves over and over again in our journey of transformation. Although it's lovely to be a butterfly now and then, our most constant experience in life is similar to that of the industrious caterpillar: We grow and change.

We may make quick changes while wearing a cape. The word *escape* comes from the word *cape.* You "throw off your cape" to make a quick getaway when needed. This versatile cape can be worn on a chilly spring day or night, and it can also convert to a short skirt.

Making and wearing this project is an embrace of life with all its change. It hugs our shoulders with the reminder that we're strong and beautiful beings of nature. There's an old Yiddish expression that says: "God gave me troubles, but he also gave me shoulders to bear them."

While knitting, I invite you to honor the spirit of change in your life. The recycled-silk yarn is alive because it was spun with a wide variety of silk pieces. It may vary in texture or color; sometimes it's thick, and sometimes it's thin. Every skein is unique, just as every life is unique. Stitch by stitch, the colors dazzle and dance under your fingers as you blend the silk with two different shades of mohair. Feel the fiber. It's empowering to literally take change into your own hands.

Let the dynamic variations of the yarn help you reflect upon the twists and turns of change in your life. Do you embrace the constancy of change? What changes have you made recently? What would you like to alter next? What new developments excite you, and which ones frighten you? What support do you need to take those steps?

Are you in the chrysalis stage right now, or are you ready to fly? Give yourself credit for all the times that you faced difficult changes with grace and determination, and forgive yourself for the times you stumbled. Just as you may rip out knitting or mistakes that don't work, you can make corrections in your life. As you create your Cape of Constant Change, surround yourself with safety, strength, and colorful vision.

(Pattern and yarn information can be found at the end of this book in the section entitled "Knitting Patterns.")

chapter 23

Binding Off: Endings and Beginnings

*"Flow into the knowledge that what you are seeking
Finishes often at the start, and, with ending, begins."*

— Rainer Maria Rilke

You've made your project the required length—you're fin-ished! It's time to "bind off" or end. The term *bind off* is also referred to as *cast off.* It's interesting to note that the word *cast* can refer to both beginning and ending a project. Like the Hebrew word *shalom,* it means hello and good-bye. Shalom also means "peace." Hopefully, you've found some peace between casting on and casting off your knitting.

Binding off is the process of ending your knitting so that the stitches don't unravel. You're literally dropping one stitch over the other in order to create a secure knotted edging. Knots are symbolic of safety. We want to protect what is valuable to us, and it's important to reinforce our hard work and positive thoughts. We find ways to prevent becoming unraveled.

Some of us have trouble letting go, and we may bind off too tightly. This can cause the stitches to break with wear. In life, if we hold on too tightly to any situation, we may squeeze the vitality out of it. Sometimes we need to say good-bye in order to begin a new journey. We may outgrow a situation just as the butterfly becomes too big for its cocoon—it must break out of its protective chrysalis and fly away.

Here's the simple, practical solution in knitting when binding off too tightly: Use bigger needles for your bind-off row, and you'll get a more elastic finish.

When we finish a project, relationship, or event, it's important to give ourselves some space and time to digest the ending. How often do we pause to assimilate an achievement or a change in our lives? Most of us jump into the next thing: We move to a new house and schedule work the next day. We finish creating a book, sweater, or painting, and immediately begin the next project. The Puritan work ethic drives us to be constantly productive, but a good farmer knows that a field needs time to be fallow so that the next season's crop can be splendid. When you eat a huge meal, you need time to digest so that you may assimilate the food that ultimately nourishes your body, in addition to savoring the experience of the meal.

What might happen if we let ourselves be nourished by our accomplishments? What if we gave ourselves the space we need to recover from a struggle or trauma? Perhaps giving ourselves time to truly integrate our endings may not only prevent us from becoming frayed and unraveled, it may actually create more energy and a positive perspective for our next adventure.

The Finishing Touch

"If a job is once begun, never leave it till it's done. Be the labor big or small, do it well or not at all." My mother used to repeat this aphorism relentlessly, which probably explains why I resisted it for years. Perhaps the harsh know-it-all tone of this homily turned me off as well. Beyond that (I reluctantly admit), it contains a kernel of good advice.

The last few hours of work on a knitted project make the difference between a sweater that looks *handmade* and one that looks *homemade.* The handmade item looks polished and skillful, while the homemade sweater has a few more rough edges.

Many people love to finish their projects. They regard the process as a puzzle and relish putting the pieces together, paying attention to every stitch of the seam in order to make it seem seamless. They weave in the messy ends of yarn and shape the garment so that it fits perfectly. This process is called "blocking." Assembling the garment with tender loving care honors the time spent working on it. It's a thrill to see our artistry emerge in the way we envisioned it, and we delight in the completion of a job well done.

Does your finishing process reflect how you tend to yourself? Do you rush through your life brushing aside your needs, or do you treat yourself with respect? Do you pay attention to the details that will help you live better? Do you integrate the fragmented parts of yourself? Do you feel that you truly *deserve* the attention that's necessary in order to be happy and healthy? Finishing a sweater with care and self-love requires that you value excellence and take yourself seriously.

Learning to finish a knitted project is a skill: You learn how to bind off, seam, block, and attend to small details. Your self-care requires the same attention. You need to tune in and assess whether you're getting enough rest, good nutrition, exercise, community time, and creative expression.

You can integrate the parts of your life with the same care and excellence you use to finish your knitting. Each time

TENDER TRANSITION

you complete a creative project, you have an opportunity to assess the progress of your skills. It's exciting to notice that you've acquired more mastery or successfully implemented new techniques. You build the confidence to try more complex designs or patterns. Most important, finishing a project with excellence makes space in your creative imagination for the next idea. By attending to the end of the journey, you make a statement about your personal value and give yourself the gift of accomplishment. The act of finishing can be a ritual of closure; it's the final chord that concludes the concert.

Here's a kinder, gentler version of my mother's aphorism:

If a job is once begun, enjoy the process. Have some fun.
Be the labor big or small, learn from doing. Give your all.

Endings and Beginnings

Once I taught a knitting class to a group of cancer survivors. I asked them about their relationship to fiber. One by one, they said that they hated to end projects. They all had a number of unfinished projects in their closets and for some reason couldn't complete them. I commiserated, since I, too, resist the seaming and blocking that's necessary to finish a sweater.

But as we discussed this topic, the room got quiet with the arrival of truth: The survivors were afraid that if they ended their projects, they would die. Having a cancer diagnosis forced them to confront the concept of ending on a daily basis. The unfinished hat for the niece, the incomplete sweater for the son or husband served as small protections from their mortality. They did *not* want endings; they wanted beginnings. But they were also frustrated, because they

233

missed the feeling of achievement that completion brings. They wanted to experience the joy of giving their handmade gift to a loved one.

Why do so many knitters hate to end projects? I sent out a questionnaire to more than 100 knitters, and a large percentage of them confided that they hate to finish their work. Someone wrote: "I get finishing anxiety when I am close to completion. I doubt everything about my project. The sweater is too small or too big, the armhole is too short, the neck is wrong. Even a simple scarf can be the source of great consternation. It might be too wide, too narrow, or maybe it's the wrong yarn. I want to avoid dealing with the ending, and yearn to start another project."

What is the source of all these (often unfounded) doubts? What are we seeking to avoid by beginning another project? A clue might exist with the word *avoid*. Do we want to avoid a void? Are we afraid of emptiness? Perhaps it's fear of loss. Endings are often sad: Something is over, and it will never be the same again. Emotions emerge. Guilt comes with recriminations about all that we did and didn't do, as well as everything that we should and shouldn't have done. Grief emerges with the ache of loss.

Ugh—who wants to feel all that? Maybe that's why so many people procrastinate. They turn a project's conclusion into a nail-biting *dead*line, or they may slap the work together haphazardly in order to "get it over with." When driven by panic and pressure to finish, how can we have time or space in our psyches to feel anything?

Yet in avoiding these emotions, we may deny ourselves the chance to experience life more intimately. Knowing that life is temporary makes it precious. What happens if we face the reality that each moment will be lost, and we dare to be in the center of it anyway? What if we're awake and aware of each moment while it's happening? We may feel truly alive.

I've never loved my cat more ardently than I do now that she is elderly. I know that each moment with Molly counts. My eyes take snapshots of her innocent sleeping beauty. My ears record her meow dialogues and engine-like purring, and my hands memorize the feel of her black-velvet fur with a profound love. Her impermanence makes me realize how much I cherish her—I've never been so close to a cat. This intimacy with Molly moves me to love others and myself with the same conviction.

In Chinese medicine, grief is associated with the lungs. These organs connect us to spirit: We inspire through our lungs. Although grief and longing are painful emotions, they bring us closer to our higher selves. It's often during our deepest tragedies that we discover our true fiber. We feel acute awareness of every moment and discover our strength, purpose, and wisdom. We find out what's important to us.

This insight may bring us to the beginning of a bold new adventure. All endings are beginnings and all beginnings are endings. When we graduate from school, the ceremony is called a "commencement," not a "termination." We begin a new chapter of life. The end of the story of knitting the sweater begins the new story of wearing it. Remember that in knitting, we find our beginning point with an *end* of yarn. We begin with one stitch and end with one stitch. We cast on again.

MOLLY'S TEA PARTY

chapter 24

A Tradition of Making Useful Objects Beautiful

"The work of the world is as common as mud. Botched, it smears the hands, crumbles to dust. But the thing worth doing well done has a shape that satisfies, clean and evident. Greek amphoras for wine or oil, Hopi vases that held corn, are put in museums but you know they were made to be used. The pitcher cries for water to carry and a person for work that is real."

— Marge Piercy

As you sit down to knit, remember that you're connected to the millions of knitters whose hands have held yarn and needles and whose hearts have knit love into billions of stitches. Knitting is an old tradition of comfort and loveliness. Making useful objects beautiful is a practice that elevates your everyday living to art. It's a way of honoring every detail you encounter as you live your day-to-day life: the hat that warms your head as you shovel the driveway, the gloves that enable you to work in the garden on a chilly autumn Sunday, and the socks that keep your feet dry when you're unexpectedly caught in the rain.

Many cultures regard the creative act of filling their world with handcrafted objects as sacred. The Balinese make a napkin gorgeous, and Native Americans decorate every object in their homes. The Amish create their quilts from used clothing so that nothing is wasted. All resources, efforts, and time are valuable. Beauty doesn't have to be removed from us in museums and galleries. We can value it every day to give our lives meaning and grace.

What do you cherish? Yes, the Picasso hanging in the Museum of Modern Art is valuable, but the afghan your grandmother made when you were little is priceless. Why? Regardless of the afghan's colors, textures or patterns, the true treasure is the spirit of your grandmother in every stitch: her touch, her thoughts, generosity, time, and affection. Her afghan isn't just a blanket; it becomes a protective cover of love.

Making beauty in our lives is a way to reflect the wonder of nature. Nature creates beauty that is also useful: trees that shade and bear fruit, flowers that provide remedies, and spectacular sunsets that offer a visual balm to the challenges of life.

The interconnectedness of nature is awe inspiring. Everything has a purpose: An air current in Japan creates a storm in Alaska that sends weather to the southwestern United States. The climate created in the Arizona desert by that chain reaction makes a perfect environment for tubular red flowers that are attractive to hummingbirds. Those birds and those flowers aren't found elsewhere. The hummingbird carries the pollen from flower to flower, thus continuing the cycle. The fabric of life is as intertwined as the knitting in your lap, one stitch dependent on another.

We need to be connected to each other and the earth. Do you notice how you feel the moment you arrive at the ocean, a forest, or the desert? You feel a quiet *Ah* within, a memory of *Yes, this is where I truly belong.* Just as you tie a knot on your finger to remember something, the knots on the fringes of a prayer shawl and those between the mala beads are meant to help you remember that you, too, are part of something larger. You're a stitch in the fabric of the world.

There's a tendency to seek comfort from knitting during troubled times. While at Valley Forge, future first lady Martha Washington formed knitting circles to make socks and bandages. The Red Cross organized scores of women who "knit their bit" for the servicemen during the two world wars. And it's no coincidence that after September 11, 2001, there was a surge of interest in fiber and knitting.

Life-shaking events rattle our roots and reminded us of the fragility of life. Difficult times teach us the vital importance of living fully and appreciating every moment. When everything around us feels as if it's coming unraveled, we're reminded of the deeply essential and comforting tradition of making connections to others and ourselves. We want to touch something soft and make something beautiful. By using our hands, we can feel a little more in charge of a piece of the world—we may knit our lives back together.

In the old days, we knitted because we needed the scarf, gloves, and sweater to keep us warm when the weather was cold. They were necessities. In this day of the Internet, malls, and department stores, we can easily buy a scarf. And since many of us consume so much and have so many things in our closets already, these knitted items are hardly necessities.

Perhaps the "new necessity" is in finding time to be reflective and digest our lives. Most of us hunger to find a calm respite from our activity-addicted world. Maybe what we need now is to connect with the intimate process of creation, to do something simply because the process gives us pleasure.

The handmade hat or scarf is one of a kind—there's none like it. Even if another was made from the same pattern, each knitted object was made to the sound of a unique heartbeat.

I believe the basic truth is that we're human beings with necks that will sometimes need to be protected from cold or adorned with something lovely. We have hands that want to work and make something beautiful and eyes that are curious to see progress, growth, and development. Our minds require space to ramble so that we may think new thoughts, and our imaginations crave passageways for their visions. We have hearts that need to love. What *is* essential and necessary? As we must breathe and eat to survive, we also need to find meaning and beauty in the matter of the earth.

As you sit with needles and yarn, knit in your intentions of love, peace, and hearth. Let your breath of life be in every stitch, and let your hands touch the yarn with care and comfort. Allow your dreams, hopes, and affirmations to find home in the knots. Let all your emotions be acceptable to the fabric, and permit yourself to reconcile your mistakes and "human being-ness" with laughter. As you knit, listen carefully, and you may hear the echo of countless knitting needles, clicking away the message that there's hope, kindness, beauty, and meaning in every stitch of the human tapestry.

HAT TREE

afterword

Listen to Your River

When we thought about ending our book, we were reminded of a seminal event that we experienced several years ago. We decided to include this story since it illustrates how the creative process is a remarkable journey full of uncertainty, chaos, inspiration, and joy. Sometimes life's unexpected obstacles catalyze us to call upon our inventiveness and resourcefulness.

We saw the dark stripe of cloud on the horizon and didn't think much about it. The day was clear and magnificent in the red-rock desert of southern Utah. The morning was spent hiking through the umber canyons and finding fossils. We remarked that dinosaurs might have cleared the path before us. Daena spontaneously began singing the Beatles' song "Help" in a slow, soulful chant as she walked. Wren joined in with harmonies. We were singing about getting our feet back on the ground. It was a preview of things to come.

Steaks of lightning and cracks of thunder got our attention. Was a storm rolling in? It was already 3 P.M., and we knew that we should be driving our Jeep out of the canyon in order to get to the highway before dark. We had a long, rocky, unpaved journey ahead of us.

As we slowly made our way along the winding road, our eyes focused like laser beams on the threatening horizon. The dark stripe was quickly gobbling up the wide, azure sky. We'd heard about the danger of sudden heavy rains and flash floods in this area.

"Let's try to move the clouds with fierce intention," one of us said. We concentrated with all our might as we shouted, "Move! Go back. Don't bring us rain!" Needless to say, we lost the tug-of-war with the clouds. Suddenly, they were overhead, and we were in the middle of a torrential downpour.

The desert can be a place of stark stillness. Sometimes it's a place of dark rage. This moment was a desert temper tantrum. The flimsy canvas covering the Jeep couldn't keep the whipping rain at bay, and water came in sheets. Lightning blazed across the black sky, and thunder reverberated through the rocks. The time lapse between the flashes of lightning and the sounds of thunder was too close for comfort. The lightning strikes were nearby.

We were in it, and there was no way out. Terrified, we drove helter-skelter, struggling to find the way. Daena was at the wheel, trying to see despite the zero visibility. *So this is what they mean when they talk about flash floods.*

Suddenly, the road in front of us ceased to be a road, and became a river—a big, rushing river in a hurry to get where it was going. We gasped. *Was this how it was going to end?* The headline would read: "Two Women Dead in Flash Flood at Lavender Canyon."

No time to think. Luckily, Daena was able to get the Jeep onto an elevated patch of land. Although a running river blocked us, we were on solid ground.

Wren began ranting: "Why did we come here? Why didn't we leave earlier? No one knows we're here. We're doomed. Not only that, I have phone sessions with clients tomorrow night!" Her wails were drowned out by the sound of the pelting rain.

Time passed. Then, as suddenly as it began, the rain stopped. What now? How long would we have to wait to be able to cross this new river? How long would it take for the water to be soaked up by the thirsty soil of the desert? The river was deep and wide.

By now it was after 5 o'clock, and we wouldn't have enough time to get to the highway while it was still light. Daena got out of the Jeep and sat by the river. Wren continued muttering to herself. There was nothing to do, and we weren't going anywhere.

Daena thought that we needed to quietly observe the water. Was it still rising? The river had presented itself to us so dramatically that it seemed impolite not to listen to what it needed to say, so she meditated by its edge. She laughed as she remembered singing "Help" earlier that day. *Perfect.*

We had enough food and water to last until the next day, we had a guitar . . . and we had each other. We were soaking wet but knew the desert heat well enough to know that this was a temporary condition.

"Hey, Wren, didn't you say just yesterday that it would be great to sit by a babbling brook in the middle of the desert? Well, here's your babbling brook."

Wren laughed. The moment of her surrender was palpable. She took out the guitar and started to sing. The birds emerged from hiding and joined in. Leonard Cohen's song "Suzanne" filled the air, with its haunting lyrics about going down to the river.

Daena said, "There's no place I'd rather be than here with you." We looked around at the majesty of the red rocks, the vast blue sky, and each other. "What more do we need?"

And it was true. We'd been on an informal creativity retreat that summer. We were recharging our batteries and giving ourselves lots of creative free time to explore the various artistic forms we loved. This meeting with the river gave us a sudden opportunity to be in the moment.

But the big question loomed: How would we cross the river to get home? Daena watched the river to see if it was going down. At first it was too deep to drive through—we'd risk getting water and silt in the engine. We sat looking at the swirling torrent, observing the profound life metaphors that it offered us. It taught us about our relationship to time, control, expectations, change, and beauty. We'd never communed with a river so intimately.

"Aha, the water level is receding!" Eventually, it was about as high as the tops of the Jeep's wheels. We'd have to drive slowly enough to avoid splashing waves into the engine, but fast enough to gain some traction without getting stuck. A delicate balance would be necessary. After much deliberation about the many possible scenarios of success and failure, we simply decided to go for it. However, there was another important unknown: How deep was the center of the river? We knew the depth at the edges, but was there an unseen ledge beneath the water? Had the flood deposited any boulders that we couldn't see?

The moment we finally decided to crank the engine and go forward felt like the last scene from the film *Thelma & Louise*. We took a deep breath and nodded at each other: It was time to go home. Daena stepped on the gas pedal and the clutch carefully, trying to be sure that we wouldn't stall midway through. Suddenly we were *inside* the river we'd been watching so intently. We were moving like an old-time riverboat, parting the waters with steady, deliberate momentum.

Simultaneously, we both realized that we were going to make it through just fine, and we hooted with delight. The experience was exhilarating. When we reached the other side, we found the road easily. The light of a full moon illuminated our path. Our burning need to get back before sunset gave way to a deep appreciation for the unplanned nighttime journey that became a magical and unforgettable experience.

That flash flood brought us a holy mess of creative process. It plucked us out of our certainty and deposited us in the middle of the unknown. We encountered confusion, fear, resistance, feelings of chaos, and sublime surrender. We had to figure out how to get out of our tangle with nature while observing our habitual patterns, and we discovered the challenge of untying more than one wet knot.

As we meditated on the "right" time to go, we realized that there was no right time. We would go when we all felt ready—Daena, Wren, and the river. We were listening to the cycles of our creative imagination as we brainstormed about various solutions to our problem. We listened, laughed, and had more than one visit from the inner critic. We learned about the difference between intentions and tension. We sang, danced, and created poetry. Life metaphors were everywhere, waiting to be discovered.

We offer this tale to you as a touchstone for your creative process. May your journey be filled with many opportunities for you to love, respect, and enjoy your magnificent creative rivers.

RIVER GUIDE

Knitting Patterns

Seeds of Intention Scarf

(Three versions)

designed by Wren Ross

I've included three versions of my Seeds of Intention Scarf pattern. The first version uses the seed stitch, which requires that you be comfortable with both the knit and purl stitch. The second version is a simple garter stitch, which is perfect for beginning knitters. It uses a plain knit stitch throughout the scarf. The third version is a Möbius strip, which has a very interesting shape. It's easy to make, and you may choose to use either garter or seed stitch.

At the end of each pattern, you'll find information about the yarn used in the design. You may find these fine yarns and all the supplies you need at your local yarn store. To see color potos of each design visit **www.wrenross.com**

Materials:
Yarn
Version #1: "Rowan Big Wool," (100% merino wool; 87 yds [80m] 100g): #001 "White Hot"—2 skeins
Version #2: "Rowan Ribbon Twist," (70% wool, 25% acrylic, 5% Polyamide; 66 yds [60m]): #115 "Rapid"—2 skeins
Version #3: Classic Elite "Bravo," (40% rayon, 35% mohair, 13% silk, 6% wool, 6% nylon; 48 yds [44m]): #3701 "Mist," or #3733 "Frost"—2 skeins

Needles
Size 17 (12.75 mm)
Crochet hook—size M (9mm)

Finished Measurements

Version 1: 9" (23 cm) w x 49" (125 cm) l

Version 2: 9" (23cm) w x 40" (102 cm) l

Version 3: 8" (20 cm) w x 36" (92 cm) l

Tip: You can make a neater edge on your scarf by slipping the first stitch. Just insert the tip of your right needle purl wise into the first stitch on the left needle, and slip it over to the right needle without knitting it.

Note: This is called a "selvage stitch" or edge stitch. The word *selvage* means "self-edge."

Abbreviations:

K—knit

P—purl

Sl1P—slip the stitch as if to purl from the left needle to the right needle

GS—garter stitch, knit every stitch

BO—bind off

Stitch Pattern:

Seed Stitch: Row 1: Sl1P, K1 *P1, K1, repeat from * until 2 stitches before end, K2.

Repeat row 1 for pattern. This stitch is worked on an odd number of stitches.

Edge Stitch: At the beginning of each row, slip 1" stitch as if to purl (S11P).

Garter Stitch: Knit every row.

Directions:

Seeds of Intention Scarf Version #1: Seed stitch
Using Rowan Big Wool #001
Cast on 17 stitches.
Rows 1–4: Sl1P, work GS
Row 5: Begin seed-stitch pattern.
Repeat row 5 until scarf measures 49" (125 cm) or desired
    length.
Repeat rows 1–4.
BO all stitches in pattern. Weave in ends.

You may choose to put fringe on your scarf. I recommend using fluffy mohair yarn. (I used Classic Elite's Bravo #3701.) Cut approximately 12 lengths of yarn measuring 28" (71 cm) each. Fold each length in half and insert crochet hook from wrong side of work through a stitch at the scarf edge. Bring center of strands through the stitch to form a loop. Tighten knot. Place evenly, one stitch apart.

Note: In the Kabbalah, the fringe (or *tzitzit*) on the prayer shawl represents the Divine energy strands that flow from the infinite.

Seeds of Intention Scarf Version #2: Garter Stitch
Using Rowan Ribbon Twist #115
Cast on 17 stitches.
Sl1P, work GS.
Continue until scarf measures 49" (125 cm) or desired
    length.
BO all stitches in pattern.
Optional: Affix fringe using method for version #1.

Seeds of Intention Scarf Version #3: Möbius

Another version of the Seeds of Intention Scarf is a Möbius strip. This is a continuous, one-sided surface that was named after the German mathematician and astronomer August Ferdinand Möbius (1790–1868). Mathematicians who study knot theory use this device to examine shapes. A Möbius strip represents infinity because it has no beginning or end—that's why it's often used as a symbol for recycling.

Directions:

Using Classic Elite "Bravo" #3701 "Mist," or #3733 "Frost" Cast on 17 stitches.

Sl1P, work seed stitch until scarf measures 36" (92 cm) (or desired length). Make a half twist and sew the seams together.

Resources

The beautiful yarns chosen for these patterns come from the following manufacturers. You may contact them to find out where these yarns are sold in your area. Visit your local yarn shop for knitting needles and any other accessories.

Rowan USA at Westminster Fibers, Inc.
4 Townsend West, Unit 8
Nashua, NH 03063
Phone: (800) 455-9276
Fax: (603) 886-1056
www.knitrowan.com

Classic Elite Yarns
122 Western Avenue
Lowell, MA 01851-1434
Phone: (978) 453-2837
Fax: (978) 452-3085
www.classiceliteyarns.com

Cape of Constant Change

Designed by Wren Ross

<u>Materials:</u>
Yarn

Main Color (MC)—Himalaya Yarn Recycled Silk (100% silk,
80 yds, 100g): "Tibet"—4 hanks

Contrasting Color (CC1)—Classic Elite La Gran Mohair
(76.5% mohair, 17.5% wool, 6% nylon; 90 yd [82m]
1.5 oz): #6555 "Infra-Red"—1 skein

Contrasting Color (CC2)—Classic Elite La Gran Mohair
(76.5% mohair, 17.5% wool, 6% nylon; 90 yd [82m]
1.5 oz): #6546 "Azure"—1 skein

Needles
Size 15 (10 mm): 29" (80cm) circular. Adjust needle size if
  necessary to obtain the correct gauge.

Notions
Stitch markers

Gauge
9 sts = 4" (10 cm)
12 rows = 4" (10 cm)

Finished Measurements
  One size fits most. Worked from the top edge down; the
cape is approximately 13" l (33 cm) and approximately 34"
w (86cm) at top edge and 60" w (153 cm) at bottom edge.

Color Pattern:
4 rows—one strand of MC and CC1 held together.
2 rows—two strands of MC held together.
4 rows—one strand of MC and CC2 held together.
2 rows—two strands of MC held together.

Edge Stitch: At the beginning of each row, work the Slip 1 as
if to purl.

  Note: Work with 2 strands of yarn held together throughout, as specified in stitch pattern.
  Color Pattern: You're invited to use your creative intuition to make different striping patterns or even a pattern of
randomness! Trust. Enjoy. It will work. But remember, if you
change the repeat of rows, it could result in different yarn
requirements.

Abbreviations:

K—knit

P—purl

Sl1P—slip one stitch as if to purl

Pm—place marker

St st—Stockinette stitch. Knit 1 row, purl 1 row.

GS—garter stitch. Knit every row.

Inc—"lifted" Increase 1 stitch by knitting into loop at base of stitch.

RS—right side

WS—wrong side

Tog—together

St—stitch

Directions:

With 1 strand of MC and 1 strand of CC1 held tog, loosely cast on 55 stitches. Starting with row 1 of Color Pattern:

Row 1: Sl1P, K1, increase 1 st, knit to 3 st before end, inc 1, knit 3.—57 stitches.

Rows 2–3: Repeat row 1. (4 stitches increased)—61 stitches.

Row 4: Set up markers. Sl1P, K 5, *pm, k7,* repeat from * to * a total of 7 times, pm, K6. (8 markers placed.) Note: Slip each marker from left needle to right needle as you come to it.

Row 5: (First increase row) Sl1P, K4, *(inc 1, slip marker, knit to 1st before next marker)* repeat from * to * ending with inc 1, k 6 —(69 sts).

Row 6 and all even rows: Sl1P, K 5, purl (slipping markers) to 6 sts remaining, k 6.

Row 7 & 8: Work as for row 5 and 6 except on the RS row, pass markers, but do not increase.

Row 9: Second increase row: Sl1P, K to one stitch before marker, inc1, slip marker, inc 1. Now you are making increases 1 stitch before and 1 after markers. (16 stitches increased)—85stitches.

Row 10–12: Work even in St st, maintaining first and last 6 stitches in garter border.

Repeat rows 9 through 12 increasing every 4th row until you have 133 stitches.

Work even, maintaining 6 sts at beginning and end of each row in GS until cape is 11" (28 cm) from cast on edge.

Work bottom edge in GS as follows:

Knit 2 rows using 2 strands of MC held together.

Knit 2 rows MC and CC2 held together.

Knit 2 rows using 2 strands of MC held together.

Loosely bind off all stitches and weave in ends.

Wrap right side over left and place shawl pin at the top edge to secure cape.

Resources

The beautiful yarns chosen for this pattern come from the following manufacturers. You may contact them to find out where these yarns are sold in your area. Visit your local yarn shop for knitting needles and any other accessories.

Classic Elite Yarns
122 Western Avenue
Lowell, MA 01851-1434
Phone: (978) 453-2837
Fax: (978) 452-3085
www.classiceliteyarns.com

HimalayaYarn
149 Mallard Dr.
Colchester, VT 05446
Phone: (802) 862-6985
Fax: (802) 658-6274
www.HimalayaYarn.com

The Shawl pin shown on the *Cape of Constant Change* may be obtained from:

Cats and Cobwebs
P.O. Box 1555
Duarte, Ca 91009-4555
Phone/Fax: (626) 303-0543
www.artsights.com/cobwebs
cobwebs@pacificnet.net

MORNING STAR

Your Creativity Journal

your creativity journal

As you begin to write in the following pages of *Your Creativity Journal,* you might want to use the photos in this book as a springboard for your exploration of the creative process. We call this streaming exercise a *photo dialogue,* which can be expressed through writing, contemplation, painting, sculpting, dancing, acting, or your favorite artistic form.

It's helpful to begin your photo dialogue by posing some questions that open your mind and engage your curiosity. We've provided some sample questions for you to consider as you look at the images. Feel free to come up with your own ideas and observations as you explore each photo.

Chapter 1 p. 7 *Journey:*

How does the winding road in this image reflect your creative process?

Imagine this is a frame in a film. What happens next? Who might be traveling on this road and why?

If you imagine *yourself* as an adventurer who is traveling on that route, what might you be thinking, seeing, hearing, and feeling?

Chapter 1 p. 13 *Wish:*

As a child, you may remember gently blowing these tiny seeds into the world as you made a wish. When you think about your dreams and current aspirations, what seeds of intention might you cast forth now?

Write a poem about the delicate innocence of this plant.

Chapter 2 p. 27 *Rock Art Birth:*

Imagine the event that might have inspired this rock art.

How does this image of birth reflect what is being born within you at this moment?

Chapter 3 p. 37 *Shadow Play:*

What thoughts, feelings, or impulses arise as you look at this photo?

What is the hand in this shadow reaching for?

Chapter 4 p. 50 *Steps:*

As you look at these ancient stairs, imagine the people who walked upon them. If they were alive today, what wisdom might they pass on to you?

Chapter 5 p. 55 *Timeless Vessel:*

Tell the story of the making of this vessel. Who made it and for what purpose?

What would you like to place in this container?

Imagine that this bowl can speak. What might it say to you about your creative process?

Chapter 5 p. 60 *Moment:*

Have you ever been in a place in nature that reminds you of this image? When was it? What were you doing? How did you feel? What sounds did you hear?

As you look at the sparkling interplay of light and water in this photo, create a poem, song, painting, or knitted garment that conveys your experience.

Chapter 6 p. 62 *Twilight Dance:*

What is evoked within you as you look at this image? What gestures or sounds does this photo inspire you to make?

What is the tree expressing?

Chapter 6 p. 69 *Other World:*

Imagine yourself walking amidst these wind-carved shapes. Where have you come from and where are you going?

If these rock formations were a community of beings huddled together, what might they be whispering to each other?

Chapter 6 p. 77 *Impermanence:*

The creative process involves cycles of construction and destruction. Tell the story of this ancient edifice as it changed over time, from its beginnings as an idea in the mind of an architect to its current condition as ruins visited by modern tourists. Try telling the story from the building's point of view.

Chapter 7 p. 90 *Tenacity:*

If this desert plant could think, what might its secret inner thoughts be?

How does this image embody a stage in your creative path?

Chapter 8 p. 94 *Perspective:*

What do you see in this image? What does this meeting of rock and sky inspire in you? Where would you place yourself in this scene?

Chapter 9 p. 101 *Web Sight:*

Imagine yourself as a spider who is delicately navigating along the web of your creative process. Remember that each spider spins its network of thread from the substance of its own body and has everything it needs within itself. As you create, how are you similar to the spider?

If the spider in this image could speak, what words of advice might it give you?

Chapter 10 p. 110 *Narrow Passage:*

What tight passageway or resistance are you encountering in your life lately?

What might be on the other side of this narrow crevice? When you look at this picture, how do you feel? If you imagine yourself standing between the two walls with your arms outstretched, what might you want to say? What do the walls represent in your creative process or your life?

Chapter 11 p. 115 *Deep Breadth:*

What feelings or sensations arise as you gaze at the expanse of this setting?

Imagine that someone is just about to enter this scene. Where have they come from and why are they here? Are they alone or do they have company?

Chapter 11 p. 121 *Cloud Stories:*

As a child, did you ever lie on your back watching the changing shapes of clouds tell a tale? As you look at this photo, what figures or story do you see?

Now imagine that you're somebody from another time in history looking up at this sky. Who are you? Where are you? What's happening in your life?

Chapter 11 p. 126 *Inner Light:*

Imagine that this flower can speak. What might it say to you about your creative process?

Chapter 12 p. 133 *Stage Presence:*

As you contemplate this image, listen to the echoes of the first words uttered in this amphitheater. Who said these words and why?

If you were to enter the stage and stand on the center rock, what soliloquy would you give? Who do you see in the audience?

Chapter 13 p. 137 *Invitation:*

Think of this bridge as a transition you're facing in your life right now. If you imagine yourself walking onto the bridge, ask yourself what you need to bring with you on your journey. What do you hope is on the other side of the bridge?

Chapter 14 p. 147 *Passing It On:*

What story do you see unfolding in this image? Who are the people? How do they know each other? What are they saying?

What would you like to pass on to a child in your life?

Chapter 16 p. 167 *Optimism:*

Create a painting that includes this flower. What colors would you use?

If you decided to pick this flower, who would you give it to? Write some song lyrics to accompany your gift.

Chapter 17 p. 172 *Still Standing:*

Which stage in your creative process is best described by this image? What do the pillars and other stone remnants represent in your story?

Chapter 17 p. 175 *Starting Point:*

What do these hands evoke in your imagination? What dialogue do you hear?

What does this image say to you about the experience of learning a new skill?

Chapter 18 p. 182 *Needle Mania:*

Imagine that each of these knitting needles has a voice and something to express. What are they gossiping about?

Chapter 19 p. 184 *Knitting Meditation:*

Write or speak aloud this person's thoughts in a stream of consciousness.

Chapter 21 p. 213 *Tangle:*

What feelings or movements does this image catalyze in you?

As you look at this photo, does it remind you of a situation in your life?

Chapter 23 p. 232 *Tender Transition:*

Place yourself inside this image. What are you thinking and anticipating? Imagine that it's a day in the future. What might your diary entry be that day?

Chapter 23 p. 236 *Molly's Tea Party:*

As you look at this picture, tell the story of what happens next.

Chapter 24 p. 241 *Hat Tree:*

Invent a comedy sketch or children's story based on this photo. Let your imagination run free. Give yourself permission to be silly and playful.

Afterword p. 248 *River Guide:*

Imagine that you're a character in a novel who is traveling along this river. Who are you? Why are you here? Are you alone? Where are you going? What is the story of your journey?

How does this image reflect your current creative process?

Your Creativity Journal . . .

*"Today, like every other day, we wake up empty
and frightened. Don't open the door to the study
and begin reading. Take down a musical instrument.*

*Let the beauty we love be what we do. There are
hundreds of ways to kneel and kiss the ground."*

— Jelalluddin Rumi

Your Creativity Journal . . .

"I begin with an idea and then it becomes something else."
— Pablo Picasso

Your Creativity Journal . . .

"Imagination is the highest kite one can fly."

— Lauren Bacall

Your Creativity Journal . . .

"More grows in the garden than the gardener sows."

— Old Spanish Proverb

photographs and illustrations

Cover Photo *The Way I Feel* by Kevin Thom

Web Sight photo p. 101 by Russ Campbell

Knitting Meditation p. 184 by George Schlossnagle

All other photos in this book are by Daena Giardella.

Knot illustrations by Joni Coniglio

Daena Giardella's photographs can be purchased
as color or black and white photo cards or enlargements
at **www.daenagiardella.com**.

acknowledgments

W hat's the common thread between the creative process and knitting? They're both activities that require us to make connections, idea-by-idea and stitch-by-stitch.

This project gave us the opportunity to have many meaningful connections with people. We were privileged to have fascinating conversations about life, knots, birth, astronomy, mistakes, death, mythology, creativity, brain biochemistry, neurology, earth sciences, and physics with brilliant specialists. Each conversation gave us a college course of knowledge and a new friend. We're enormously appreciative of the chance to meet, know, and learn from everyone who contributed to this book.

We especially thank Cheryl Richardson, who helped manifest this dream. Her insight, kindness, and generosity have been invaluable. We also thank Michael Gerrish for his keen artistic eye, intelligence, and humor. Thanks to Marilyn Abraham and Sandy McGregor for their sage advice and much-valued friendship. We also thank Nanda Eagle for her healing presence and Alizon Lissance for her loving support.

Thanks to Solon Beinfeld, Ph.D., who's not only a wise, witty, and good friend, but who also introduced us to Elaine Riesenberg. We offer special thanks to Elaine for reading the manuscript faithfully with intelligence and care. We're grateful for her guidance. Thanks to Margery Beinfeld, professor of pharmacology at Tufts University School of Medicine, for her knowledge and astute observations. We also want to thank our assistant Susan Healey for her support and editorial suggestions.

Hay House is a remarkable publishing company. They walk the talk. Big thanks to Louise Hay, Reid Tracy, Jill Kramer, Jessica Vermooten, Amy Gingery, Shannon Littrell, Margarete Nielsen, Jacqui Clark, Stacy Vasil, Jeannie Liberati, John Thompson, Stacey Smith, Summer McStravick, Christy Salinas, Shelley Anderson, Tricia Breidenthal, and Ron Tillinghast. Each person we encountered was kind, helpful, and excellent at what they do.

Thanks to George Schlossnagle for permission to use the beautiful photo of the Tibetan woman knitting, and Joni Coniglio for her lovely knot illustrations. Thanks to Kevin Thom for permission to use his soulful photo on our cover, and Chris Ventzos for her excellent contribution to the cover design. Special thanks to Russ Campbell for his generous help with photo editing as well as his permission to use his wonderful spider photo.

We also want to thank all the scholars, experts, and colleagues who gave us information and guidance, including Rabbi Berel Levertov of the Santa Fe Chabad; Rabbi Ben-Zion, director emeritus, Harvard Hillel; Terry Plank, professor of earth sciences at Boston University; Dr. Gene J. Blatt, associate professor of anatomy and neurobiology at Boston University School of Medicine; Jeffrey Hughes, professor of astronomy at Boston University; Professor David Gordon Mitten, classical archaeologist at Harvard University; Carolyn Collins Petersen, science writer; LaRayne Willard of St. Joseph's Indian School; Debra Shapiro, senior producer, WCVB-TV, Boston; Veronica Valandra, director, Office of Native Concerns, Diocese of Rapid City; Ngodup Sangpo; Carrie Brezine, weaver and mathematician working on the Khipu Database Project at Harvard University; "Pudge" Kleinkauf of Women's

Flyfishing; Elana, monkess of Daily Zen; Fr. Albert Dilanni, S.M.; Emeric Meier, OTM from the Shrine of St. Anthony; Colleen McDannell, professor of history and religious studies at the University of Utah; Eric Druhv, naturalist at Miraval spa; the knitting class from Dana Farber; Kevin LaVine from the Library of Congress; Dorian Hughes and Linda Howe for their information on Celtic knots; Mary McWilliams, the Norma Jean Calderwood Curator of Islamic and Later Indian Art at Harvard University Art Museums; Dr. Steven Schram, acupuncturist and chiropractor; Bill Mueller, acupuncturist; Dorit Bat-Shalom, artist and friend; the staff at Zeff Photo Supply; and Judith Austin for inviting Wren to come to her fourth-grade knitting class.

There are many people to thank for their knowledge about knitting. What fun to compare notes and learn new techniques from master knitters! Thanks to Lucy Lee and the knitting group from Mind's Eye Yarns, Virginia McGlynn of Abbot yarns, Don and Janet Scope at Putting On the Knitz, Sean Riley and the staff of Woolcott, Martie Moreno of Taos Sunflower, Seyna Green, and Aldrich Robinson of Newbury Yarns. Special thanks to Kimberley O'Keeffe and Gail McHugh for their pattern-editing assistance.

Many yarn companies helped Wren in her hunt for the yarn used for the Cape of Constant Change and the Seeds of Intentions Scarf. We thank them for their fantastic yarns: Classic Elite, JCA, Skacel Collection, Himalaya Yarns, Bernat, Windhorse Trading Company, Rowen Westminster Fiber, and a special thanks to Cari Clement of Bond America for her good counsel.

We're grateful to all the artists and creative professionals with whom we've collaborated in theater productions over the past 25 years. We also wish to acknowledge our students and coaching clients.

Daena wishes to thank her parents, Lucy and Charles Giardella, and her brother and sister-in-law Joe and Laurie Giardella for their support and love over the years. We celebrate with great delight the new creativity guru in the Giardella clan: Joseph Dylan Giardella. His inquisitive mind, contagious enthusiasm, and bountiful love brought us much laughter and inspiration as we wrote this book.

Wren wants to thank her Aunt Roz, Uncle Irv, and all her cousins for their love and support. All those gift certificates for books were well used! Thanks to Arthur Quinn for his humor and observations. Wren appreciates Cathy Rand for her smart suggestions and support. Deep thanks to David Prendergast and Elizabeth Clement for their perception, wisdom, and compassion. And of course, we thank Molly, who kept our chairs warm during our winter writing sessions.

And finally, we deeply appreciate the enchanted land of northern New Mexico, which contains the essence of creativity. We thank our little casita, the smell of sage and piñon, the cry of the coyotes, the arroyos, mountains, and open sky for providing us with a sacred cocoon from which we can engage the magic of transformation again and again and again.

about the authors

Daena Giardella is an actor, creativity coach, motivational speaker, writer, and photographer. She's been called an "improvisation trailblazer" in the United States and abroad for her innovative one-woman theater performances, and a "master teacher" for her unique approach to teaching improvisational acting as a skill for everyday life. She designs original performances, presentations, and training seminars for organizations. Daena's talents were featured in the Oxygen television series, *The Life Makeover Project with Cheryl Richardson.* She has appeared on numerous other TV and radio programs, including the PBS series *Discovering Psychology.* She has also hosted her own radio show.
Website: **www.daenagiardella.com**

Wren Ross is a voice-over actor, singer, writer, consultant, and devoted knitwear designer. She has designed for Classic Elite Yarns, Artful Yarns, The Skacel Collection, and Himalaya Yarns. Her work has been featured in *Interweave Knits* and *Ultimate Knitting* magazines. She has created many original cabarets, including *Singing With Every Fiber,* which she performs throughout the country. Her writings about knitting have been published in two editions of *KnitLit* (Random House) and *Interweave Knits* magazine. Wren also teaches creativity workshops that empower people to find their authentic voice.

Website: **www.wrenross.com**

If you want to continue exploring your creative process with Daena Giardella and Wren Ross, visit **www.creativityin life.com** where you'll find interactive streaming exercises as well as information about upcoming events, performances, and workshops.

Hay House Titles of Related Interest

Caroline Myss' Journal of Inner Dialogue, by Caroline Myss

I Can Do It® Cards: *Affirmations for Creativity,*
by Louise L. Hay

The Love and Power Journal, by Lynn V. Andrews

Passionate People Produce: *Rekindle Your Passion
and Creativity,* by Charles Kovess

SARK's Creative Dream Game,
by SARK (a 50-card deck and guide)

Saying Yes to Change: *Essential Wisdom for Your Journey,*
by Joan Z. Borysenko, Ph.D., and Gordon F. Dveirin, Ed.D.

Self-Care Cards, by Cheryl Richardson (a 52-card deck)

The Well of Creativity,
by Julia Cameron, et al, with Michael Toms

All of the above are available at your local bookstore,
or may be ordered through Hay House.